# INSIDE
# IRS

# INSIDE
# IRS
## HOW INTERNAL REVENUE WORKS (YOU OVER)

JEFF A. SCHNEPPER

STEIN AND DAY/*Publishers*/New York

Grateful appreciation is given to *The Practical Accountant* for permission to reproduce the 1864 tax return from page 42 of the July/August 1976 issue.

First published in 1978

Printed in the United States of America
Stein and Day/*Publishers*/Scarborough House,
Briarcliff Manor, N.Y. 10510

Library of Congress Cataloging in Publication Data

Schnepper, Jeff A.
    Inside IRS.

    Bibliography: p. 224
    Includes index.
    1.   United States.   Internal Revenue Service.
I.  Title.
HJ5018.S33           353.007'24        77–16001
ISBN  0–8128–2444–X

*To*
*Barbara, my reason*
*and to*
*Brandy Rebecca, my motivation*

# CONTENTS

# PREFACE

No other single organization in American society has the impact of the Internal Revenue Service. Its powers surpass, at times, even those of the FBI. Its presence is felt every time a businessman eats lunch and asks for a receipt, and each week when the wage earner receives a check with taxes withheld. The bureaucracy we talk of as the Internal Revenue Service cannot effectively be understood independent of the tax code it seeks to enforce. This tax law—ambiguous, vexatious, and unintelligible to most taxpayers—sculptures the soul of the IRS organization. It is the root of many of the problems within that bureaucracy.

Without the help of many people this book could not have been written. I want to thank initially Sol Stein, my publisher, and Marilee Talman and Joshua Stein, my editors, for the faith they have shown in me. I want to thank those good IRS employees who helped me make this book possible and those bad IRS employees who made it interesting. I want to thank my primary researcher, Barbara Schnepper, and the students who assisted me in my research, especially Linda Grun and Terry Gyorfy, and my brothers, R. Cory Schnepper, Esq., and Michael Schnepper.

—Jeff Schnepper
*New Brunswick, 1978*

# INSIDE
# IRS

The biggest difference between death and taxes is that death doesn't get worse every time Congress meets.

# 1/THE (PRACTICALLY) UNLIMITED POWERS OF THE IRS

On the wall in the office of a well-known New Jersey tax attorney hangs a framed letter from the Internal Revenue Service. It reads as follows:

Dear Taxpayer:
  This is to inform you that we, at the Internal Revenue Service, have lost your file. Unless we find it within 30 days, you will face a $10,000 fine and a jail sentence of not less than five (5) years. Please advise.

The letter, of course, is a phony, though the paranoia it represents is real. This almost hysterical fear of the Internal Revenue Service is based on the American taxpayer's per-

1

ception of the agency as a bureaucratic inquisitor endowed with certain special powers. Many observers believe the Internal Revenue Service's powers go beyond normal constitutional limits and at times violate due process provisions and the Fifth Amendment protection against self-incrimination.

Internal Revenue Service horror stories abound. In Florida, while a one-legged handyman was working in the home of a Miami businessman, Internal Revenue Service agents rushed up and confiscated the handyman's car—despite documentary evidence provided at the time that the car did not belong to the person the Internal Revenue Service was out to get. It took six months and a federal court order to get the car back.

One man committed suicide, leaving a note to explain that he couldn't endure any more harassment from the Internal Revenue Service. His 17-year-old son, who had started working for the first time, was due a $400 tax refund. Instead of the refund, he received a notice from the Internal Revenue Service stating that his $400 had been applied to his dead father's taxes.

In Chicago, the IRS ordered Howard F. MacNeil, an accountant, to use his own money to pay taxes allegedly owed by a corporation which had been one of his clients. MacNeil proved he had no control of the corporation's affairs and could not be held liable for its debts, but the Internal Revenue Service agents insisted he pay the $36,000 that he "owed." When MacNeil refused, the IRS froze his personal bank accounts and posted signs outside his house proclaiming: "KEEP OUT. PROPERTY OF THE U.S. GOVERNMENT." MacNeil was hounded without mercy. While waiting for his case to be heard in court he lost his business and fell into debt. Eventually he was vindicated by a jury, but not before he was ruined financially.

In Tennessee a woman was recruited to inform against her businessman husband with a letter stolen from his desk by an Internal Revenue Service agent. The letter implied that he was having a romance with another woman.

One friend of the author, a United States Army chaplain, wrote to the Internal Revenue Service explaining that his wife was ill and had to undergo an expensive operation. The letter was written in December expressing his fear that on April 15 he would lack sufficient funds to pay his taxes in full. He therefore requested a meeting with an Internal Revenue Service agent to arrange a way for him to pay off his taxes over the year.

The Internal Revenue Service responded to this letter, written by a Major in the U.S. Army four months before any tax was due, before an audit, with a "jeopardy and termination assessment," freezing the man's bank account just when he needed the money for his wife's operation.

I recall a story told to me by a fellow attorney. The wife of one of his clients was stricken with polio and needed an iron lung to keep her alive. An IRS agent threatened to seize the iron lung unless taxes claimed to be due were immediately forthcoming. The panicked taxpayer paid the claimed deficiency immediately, so the threat was never put to the test.

In Kansas City, a police officer, Paul R. Campbell, halted a speeder, and started to write a ticket. The offending driver, after making the usual objections, identified himself as an Internal Revenue Service agent. When Campbell continued to write, the agent sneered: "We'll just have to check your taxes." Soon after Campbell filed his next tax return, he was ordered to report to the Internal Revenue Service for an examination.

Unable to find anything wrong with the officer's return, the Internal Revenue Service continued investigating Campbell for four months with telephone calls, letters, and additional interrogations before admitting at last that he owed them nothing. The IRS later contended that Campbell had been selected by their normal audit selection procedure. Even if true, though, one must question the potential impact of his experience on fellow Kansas City police officers. The ability to initiate an intensive tax audit is a powerful weapon in the hands of an unscrupulous agent.

What is so frightening about these stories is that in no case did the agents of the Internal Revenue Service exceed their legitimate authority. In each instance, then-current revenue statutes shielded their actions.

Legislation and court cases have allowed the Internal Revenue Service remarkable freedom in its dealings with taxpayers. Nowhere has this freedom been more readily visible, and more widely abused, than in the area of IRS "jeopardy" assessments. These administrative orders, issued by the IRS itself, permit the agency to bypass its own rules for the collection of whatever money an IRS auditor claims a taxpayer owes. The initial "jeopardy" determination is made strictly by the IRS district director's administrative decree—there is no previous judicial review. But once the agency issues it, a "jeopardy" assessment gives the Internal Revenue Service broad powers over the property of the targeted taxpayer. These summary proceedings can and in many cases do deprive the taxpayer of his ability to continue in business, pay living expenses, or even hire an attorney for defense purposes.

"Jeopardy" assessments take two forms. Both are intended for cases in which the IRS believes the taxpayer might quickly leave the country, remove or transfer his property, conceal himself or his possessions, or do anything else that might "frustrate [or jeopardize] collection of the tax." Both types of "jeopardy" assessments have traditionally been used as major weapons in the fight against organized crime, specifically gambling and narcotics. Both have been misused.

The first form is the ordinary jeopardy assessment. It is invoked only after the date on which the tax for the previous full year is due, April 15 for most taxpayers. The jeopardy assessment gives the Internal Revenue Service the power to *immediately* assess additional taxes, send a notice and demand for payment, and even to seize the taxpayer's property when the Internal Revenue Service believes that assessment or collection may be delayed.

The ordinary jeopardy assessment is merely an acceleration device. It makes payable today a tax that would normally be paid tomorrow. Made at the discretion of a district director of the Internal Revenue Service, it results in an immediate lien on all property owned by the taxpayer upon notice and demand for payment. Until the taxpayer petitions a court to decide how much tax is due, the Government may seize and hold any property on which a lien has been placed. There is no waiting period required between the time the IRS sends the notice of deficiency and the time it seizes the taxpayer's property, and in some cases, such as employment and wagering taxes, the IRS need not even send a notice of deficiency to the taxpayer before seizing his property, or need only send it within 60 days after the jeopardy assessment is made. Thus the taxpayer, without any previous notice, may be deprived of the benefit and use of any and all of his property—including his home, car, and business assets!

The second kind of jeopardy assessment is known as the "termination" assessment, which is used only to collect income taxes. Here the IRS district director may decide to terminate the taxpayer's taxable year at any time by sending a letter called a "Termination Notice." This letter demands *immediate* payment of any tax determined to be due for the terminated period. If the taxpayer does not pay up immediately, the Internal Revenue Service can seize the taxpayer's property. Any amount collected as a result of the termination assessment is credited against the tax finally determined to be due for the taxpayer's full year liability.

The termination assessment is designed for cases in

which the IRS thinks a taxpayer is about to leave the country with untaxed money, usually the profits from criminal activity. By ending the suspected criminal's taxable year, the IRS can immediately collect tax on the income, tax which might otherwise not be collected at all. But a termination assessment can also be issued against any taxpayer, at any time—and often unfairly and arbitrarily.

The Internal Revenue Code does exempt certain property from this kind of levy: (1) wearing apparel and school books; (2) fuel, furniture, and personal effects not exceeding $500 in value, if the taxpayer heads a family; (3) books and tools used in a trade, business, or profession, not in excess of $250; (4) unemployment benefits; (5) undelivered mail; (6) certain annuity and pension checks; (7) workmen's compensation; and (8) money ordered by a court of competent jurisdiction to be paid in support of minor children. Here, therefore, the unemployed worker may get through the assessment somewhat better than the working wage earner.

Moreover, the Code provides that:

(1) Any person who fails or refuses to surrender any property or rights to property, subject to levy, upon demand by the Secretary of his delegate, shall be liable in his own person and estate to the United States in a sum equal to the value of the property or rights not so surrendered . . . together with costs, and interest on such sum at the rate of 6 percent per annum from the date of such levy. Any amount (other than costs) recovered under this paragraph shall be credited against the tax liability for the collection of which such levy was made.

(2) If any person required to surrender property or rights to property fails or refuses to surrender such property or rights to property without reasonable cause, such person shall be liable for a penalty equal to 50 percent of the amount recoverable under paragraph (1). No part of such penalty shall be

credited against the tax liability for the collection of which such levy was made.

This means that if any person other than the taxpayer has in his use or custody any asset belonging to the taxpayer, he must surrender such property to the Service or be liable in his person and property for 150 percent of the assessment in question; nor can any of this be used to reduce the tax-liability. For example, if a family rents a furnished apartment from a landlord who is subjected to a termination assessment, it must turn over the furniture and equipment to the Internal Revenue Service or be subject to the penalties listed. This means also that banks, savings and loan associations, credit unions, corporations, etc., must surrender stock, deposits, or other assets belonging to the taxpayer upon demand.

In issuing jeopardy and termination assessments, the Internal Revenue Service has always computed the greatest tax liability possible. In many cases assessment was considerably greater than the actual tax liability. In a report to the Joint Committee on Internal Revenue Taxation, the General Accounting Office found that in 25 cases, in which the IRS assessed a total of $742,294, the total tax deficiency determined after audit was only 4.9 percent of that, or $36,665. Amounts assessed were at times found to be totally arbitrary. In the case of H. Kimmel, "every bit" of the taxpayer's property was seized. In other cases the assessments were based on inconclusive evidence and dropped completely.

In Missouri, Noel Smith was assessed for $550,000. The IRS later settled that assessment for less than $50,000. For one tax year he had actually paid $2,000 too much, but the statute of limitations prevented him from getting a refund.

Termination assessments are based on the law enacted in 1918 to prevent aliens from leaving the country with taxable funds. In 1924, Congress provided for ordinary jeopardy assessments to permit immediate assessment and collection of taxes without the delay of court proceedings.

Clearly, the jeopardy and termination assessments are powerful weapons available to the Internal Revenue Service in its enforcement of the tax laws. Jeopardy procedures can be an invaluable tool in cases where there is significant danger of evasion or escape. But these well-intentioned procedures are commonly misused, resulting in injustices such as those described above.

Even though federal courts have ruled several times that the IRS did exceed its authority in jeopardy assessment cases, the courts have usually held that a jeopardy determination is *not reviewable* when made—thus permitting the IRS to seize property before the taxpayer can present a case in court.

The rationale for this view can be found in *Springer* v. *United States,* a case the Supreme Court decided in 1880, a third of a century before the birth of the income tax:

The prompt payment of taxes is always important to the public welfare. It may be vital to the existence of the government. The idea that every taxpayer is entitled to the delays of litigation is unreasonable.

Another Supreme Court decision a few years earlier in 1875, *Taylor* v. *Secor,* paved the way for this view:

... the payment of taxes has to be enforced by summary and stringent means against a reluctant and often adverse sentiment, and to do this, modes of procedure, other than those which belong to courts of justice, are necessary.

Acting in response to criticism of how the IRS used "jeopardy" and "termination" assessments, a Senate subcommittee held hearings on the subject in November 1975. The Senate Finance Committee Subcommittee on Administration of the Internal Revenue Code set out to ". . . review these powers to insure that there are adequate safeguards to prevent those who are charged with the responsibility of administering these provisions from depriving people of their property without observing the basic constitutional requirements of due process."

The committee collected case histories of assessments based on illegal wiretap evidence, unsupported statements from informants, and sometimes, no justification at all. Jeopardy assessments not otherwise justified by the circumstances were found to have been used as a club to extract from a taxpayer an agreement to extend the statute of limitations when an audit was incomplete. Termination assessments were applied without basis as well.

In one reported instance a taxpayer's house and automobile had been seized based upon what was found to be a "patently arbitrary and capricious assessment of $244,314." Phoenix Federal District Court Judge Walter E. Craig was quoted in that case as saying "it taxes the credulity of the Court, and I suspect any reasonable court, to give any merit to the method of calculation and the computation worksheet."

In one case reported to the committee, a French citizen had been served with a termination and jeopardy assessment of $247,500 when the plane in which he was a passenger landed in New York on its way to Switzerland.

The revenue agent in that case testified that he did not know whether the Frenchman had earned any income in the United States. The agent knew only that the Frenchman was found with the money at the airport and had refused to answer certain questions. The agent testified that he had been instructed to prepare a return showing a tax due of approximately $247,500 and had done so. He admitted that the cost of living figure he had used was a pure fiction. Why was the figure $247,500 picked? That was how much cash the Frenchman had carried with him on the airplane.

The committee also discussed the case of Ed McCanse which had already received national attention through ABC-TV's "Close-Up" program. McCanse's bout with the IRS began in July 1964 when he and his two daughters sold their ranch and farming property for $960,000. Thirty percent of the purchase price was paid in cash, with the rest to be paid in installments. During the latter part of 1965 he and his daughters were audited by the Internal Revenue Service. As a result of that audit, the Internal Revenue Service claimed McCanse owed $119,000 in taxes and placed a jeopardy assessment against him. The agency issued the assessment without any warning, written or verbal; nor were any reasons or explanations later forthcoming. Almost four years after the assessment, the claim was made that the Internal Revenue Service had feared McCanse was planning to move to Canada to avoid paying his taxes. He had then been living in the same house in Oregon for almost 30 years. In 1975, during the Senate hearings, ten years after the initial audit, McCanse was still in that same house.

At the time of the jeopardy assessment, McCanse owned 50 percent of the stock of the Ronde Valley Lumber Company. The Internal Revenue Service seized his bank account and threatened to sell that stock to pay the $119,000 in taxes he allegedly owed on the installment sale of the ranch and farming property. McCanse was given one out: 40 days in which he could either pay the alleged deficiency or post a bond to insure payment.

Posting a bond after a jeopardy assessment, though, is almost impossible. Bail bondsmen require security for their loans. But usually, any property of worth the taxpayer might have had to use for security has already been seized by the Internal Revenue Service.

McCanse therefore went to his partner, C. W. Hoffman,

for help. According to McCanse, Hoffman agreed to loan him the $119,000 he needed for the bond if McCanse would put up three-fourths of his stock in their lumber company as security. McCanse claimed that Hoffman told him the transaction would be temporarily treated as a sale but assured him that he could have the stock back any time he repaid the loan.

Three and one-half years later, after extensive litigation, the Internal Revenue Service agreed that McCanse was right and returned his $119,000. In the interim, though, he had paid over $90,000 to attorneys, accountants, and appraisers. Furthermore, Hoffman then refused to return his stock, claiming that the contract clearly specified that it was a sale.

McCanse sued Hoffman to recover his stock, but the case was settled before trial with Hoffman buying McCanse's remaining one-eighth interest in the company for $350,000. McCanse had thus been forced by the Internal Revenue Service to let go of over $1 million worth of stock for $119,-000. This was in addition to a terrific toll in money and health.

The Internal Revenue Service internal administrative guidelines, as well as the tax law itself, would have prevented the actual sale of McCanse's stock before the tax court ruled on his case. McCanse, though, like other taxpayers, did not have access to the agency's internal guidelines, and an agent had threatened to sell the stock.

Fear of the Internal Revenue Service is based not only on the agency's abuse of "jeopardy" and "termination" assessments, but also on its well-earned reputation for inconsistency and unpredictability. According to a study commissioned by the Federal Administrative Conference, the Internal Revenue Service has been "whimsical, inconsistent, unpredictable, and highly personal," in dealing with those caught in its machinery. The study concluded, among other things, that different Internal Revenue Service districts follow different rules and that the same district can be either easy or tough depending on whether it is ahead of or behind its unacknowledged "quota" for recoveries.

For example, a New Yorker's chances of being audited averaged 1 in 39, compared to 1 in 78 in New Mexico. Internal Revenue Service audit negotiators in Brooklyn averaged 32 cents on the dollar in settling disputes while those in Baltimore extracted 74 cents. In Albany, New York, six of every ten delinquent accounts led to tax seizures, but only three of ten did in New Mexico. The uneven enforcement of our revenue laws becomes even more obvious in light of these 1972 figures:

## TYPE OF AUDIT INVOLVED

|  | Chance of an Audit | Field | Office |
|---|---|---|---|
| All Individual and Fiduciary | 1 in 57 | 20% | 80% |
| Non-Business $50,000 and over | 1 in 8 | 86% | 14% |
| Business $30,000 and over | 1 in 8 | 93% | 7% |
| Corporation | 1 in 14 | 100% | — |

### Odds of Being Audited—Various Districts

|  | Individuals | Corporations |
|---|---|---|
| Manhattan, N.Y. | 1 out of 37 | 1 out of 26 |
| San Francisco, Calif. | 1 out of 59 | 1 out of 9 |
| Reno, Nev. | 1 out of 33 | 1 out of 15 |
| New Orleans, La. | 1 out of 52 | 1 out of 15 |

According to Louise Brown of the Public Citizen Tax Reform Research Group, the Internal Revenue Service has not even "troubled to find out whether the statistics show patterns of uneven enforcement." Inequitable administration has certainly been indicated.

The Federal Administrative Conference also found that the higher the deficiency that the Internal Revenue Service claimed, the lower the percentage it finally accepted in settlement. The conference suggested that this was due to the ability of rich taxpayers to hire lawyers to argue their case while poorer taxpayers had no choice but to pay up. Clearly, each taxpayer did not receive exactly the same treatment, under the same rules, with the same degree of diligence.

The taxpayer's fear is further compounded by the tax law itself. He presently faces codes, regulations, and revenue manuals filling over 32 shelf feet with an incredible 40,000 pages of the most arcane, unintelligible gobbledygook ever created by an American legislature.

Most libraries seem to shelve income tax regulations in a back room somewhere between books on integral calculus and original Greek manuscripts. Internal Revenue Service training school manuals state that ". . . after obtaining and using Internal Revenue Service in-house manuals, agents can find errors in 99.9 percent of all returns if they want to."

Even so-called "tax experts" are overwhelmed. Recent nationwide spot audits by the Internal Revenue Service have documented an average 75 percent error rate on tax returns filed by paid preparers. A study commissioned by the California Department of Consumer Affairs confirms chronic tax preparer incompetence or, at best, inability. The California study covered hundreds of trained independent and franchise tax preparers randomly selected by surveyors posing as middle income taxpayers during the 1976 tax season. It found: "Only 3 out of almost 400 test returns, a figure of less than 1 percent, were correctly computed."

On the federal returns, 77.4 percent of the hypothetical

taxpayers lost refunds to which they were legally entitled. Of these cases, 86.6 percent reported unclaimed refunds between $50 and $500, while 63.2 percent lost $200 to $500.

Half the test returns did not include all necessary forms. Nearly 40 percent did not include all the information required by tax regulations.

Most interesting of all, in a comparison study, Internal Revenue Service employees were found to be almost as inaccurate as the commercial preparers. In the middle income group, they turned out a startling 79 percent error rate.

Senator Warren Magnuson of Washington related the story of a widow whose return was prepared by an agent who "unknowingly" overcharged her $775. When she discovered the error she was told that her money could not be returned because the period for making refunds had expired!

Furthermore, had the agent charged her too little, and caught his mistake within the normal three-year statute of limitations, even though her return had been *prepared by the Internal Revenue Service itself*, she would still be liable for interest on the money owed and, in some cases, a penalty as well.

Taxpayers who relied on the Internal Revenue Service Taxpayer Assistance Program for aid in the preparation of their returns have too often encountered similar problems. The argument of the Internal Revenue Service is simple. The true tax was higher. Therefore the taxpayer should pay the higher amount. As the taxpayer had the use of the extra money beyond the original due date, he or she should also pay the interest due. As in the story told by Senator Magnuson, the error must be excused according to the IRS "on the ground that agents cannot be expected to understand completely the complexities of the Code."

A study by Ralph Nader's Tax Reform Research Group confirmed that Revenue Code complexity can lead to inconsistent results. The group prepared 22 identical tax reports based on the fictional economic plight of a married couple with one child. These 22 identical copies were submitted to 22 different Internal Revenue Service offices around the country.

Each office came up with an entirely different tax figure. The results varied from a refund of $811.96 recommended by the Internal Revenue Service office in Flushing, New York, to a tax due figure of $52.14 arrived at by the Internal Revenue Service tax office in Portland, Oregon. If the law is so difficult, so complex and convoluted that the specially trained agents of the Internal Revenue Service itself cannot translate it with some degree of consistency, it is no wonder that the average American taxpayer fears he is walking on very shaky ground during his encounters with federal income tax law.

Even if "jeopardy" and "termination" assessments had never been invented, and even if the tax code were a perfectly unambiguous document, American taxpayers would still have a very good reason to fear the Internal Revenue Service: the agency uses an unofficial "quota" system in its administration of the tax laws. Though modern tax collectors are theoretically no longer paid on the basis of what they collect, success in the Internal Revenue Service hierarchy is more quickly and easily achieved by producing a huge assessment than by ordering a hefty refund.

In January 1968, Vincent Connery, president of the National Association of Internal Revenue Employees, testified on this issue during a hearing before a subcommittee of the United States Senate Judiciary Committee. Though the commissioner of the Internal Revenue Service had publicly denied the existence of quotas, Connery told the Senate subcommittee:

... it is our considered judgment that certain Internal Revenue Service management policies and procedures tend to generate a climate in which offensive practices may well take root and flourish. We have in mind specifically management's

emphasis on quotas and production goals. The pressure beginning in Washington is being transmitted to the districts
through the regional pipelines, and is vented on the working
agent and revenue officer.

He said agents were expected to show a certain amount of
"production," IRS jargon for cases completed and money
collected. When asked about the relationship between "production" and promotions, Connery responded:

Many of the employees are under the impression that if you
turn in quite a few cases more than the other people, . . . this
will come to the attention, of course, of the supervisors who
make these [promotion] recommendations, and certainly I
think you can realize that it would not hurt any revenue agent
to turn in a large tax deficiency.

Actually that . . . would meet with the approbation of all concerned, your supervisor certainly. It is just generally thought
in agency circles that to turn in a large deficiency—there is
more credit that comes your way than to turn in a recommendation for a large refund.

Before the hearing, the Internal Revenue Service administration categorically denied that the agency uses quotas.
IRS representatives contend that promotion of agents is
based solely on an overall evaluation of their work. Yet the
Internal Revenue Service admits the use of national, regional, and district "production goals." It admits that local
supervisors sometimes do "keep book" on employees and
make production comparisons.

Philip Long of Bellevue, Washington, whose judicial vic-
tories opened up many secret IRS files under the Freedom of
Information Act, testified before a later Senate inquiry. He
alleged that each year top Internal Revenue Service administrators establish a "target goal" of additional revenue that

its auditors must "produce" during the year, and that this goal is then broken down by "what amount should be taken from each taxpayer income bracket, business category, and area of the country." This, he said, is known in-house as the Internal Revenue Service "long range plan" or "program and financial plan."

During 1972, for instance, he said the plan called for office audits to produce from $68 to $71 in added revenue on each audited taxpayer with earnings of $10,000 or less, while anyone audited whose income ranged between $10,000 and $30,000 was "targeted" for an additional $926 in taxes. Small corporations, those with assets of under $250,000, would each pay an extra $1,000, and firms with assets of about $500,000 "were put down for an expected tax deficiency of $2,990."

Whether these were in fact quotas or merely budgeted expectations is beside the point. As former Internal Revenue Service agent Connery pointed out:

Under such a system, quality of performance is a casualty, and in too many cases the taxpayer may be a victim of an overzealous agent or officer frantically trying to meet his quantitative goals or quotas imposed on him from higher up in the Internal Revenue Service management structure. When talking to Internal Revenue Service employees, and even management officials, we frequently find them using the term "statistical rat race" to describe this particular setup.

When all these elements—quotas, audit disparities, unintelligible tax rules and regulations—are combined with the special surprise ingredient of financially debilitating jeopardy assessments, the resultant mixture quickly and surely induces paranoia in even the most law-abiding American taxpayers.

# 2/ "WHY ME?" HOW TAXPAYERS ARE PICKED FOR AUDIT

The envelope is nervously ripped open and the personalized letter written and addressed by a computer is fearfully read. It's from the Internal Revenue Service—greetings and an invitation to come down to the federal building for a review of your tax return. No RSVP necessary. It's a command performance and of the two thoughts that quickly come to mind the only one suitable for print is "why me?"

To answer that question, it is necessary to trace exactly what happens to an "average" individual tax return, since making your return indistinguishable from this "average" can lessen your chance of facing an audit. Once the taxpayer has prepared and signed the return, he mails it to the IRS

Regional Service Center for his geographical area. The Regional Service Center checks some of the figures and transfers all information to magnetic tape, which then goes to the IRS Computer Center in Martinsburg, West Virginia. Here, it becomes part of a Master File for the Internal Revenue Service·s complex Automatic Data Processing system, which computerizes tax data from over 120 million returns each year. With it, the Internal Revenue Service can locate people who fail to file returns and taxpayers who do not report income such as dividends or bank interest.

Using the taxpayer·s social security number for identification, the computer system also prints out notices and letters to advise a taxpayer of a tax or refund due, to request information, or to report actions taken on returns already filed and the status of a taxpayer·s account. Among many other things, it can also print out a transcript listing all transactions posted to a specific taxpayer account or for a specific taxpayer return. It is this advanced computer system that decides which returns should be audited.

First all income tax returns receive a computer examination for mathematical errors. Mistakes in addition, subtraction, multiplication, or in transferring figures from one schedule to another—for example, the total of itemized deductions to the schedule 1040—result in an immediate correction notice. If the error led to a tax deficiency, the taxpayer automatically receives a bill for that amount. If the taxpayer overpaid, the excess is applied to future installments of tax, credited, or refunded at the taxpayer's request. The taxpayer cannot appeal such corrections but can ask in writing that they be reviewed. In 1975, about 9 percent of the returns filed had mathematical errors, of which 3.1 million were in favor of the government and 3.9 million in favor of the taxpayer. By themselves, errors in arithmetic rarely lead to a full audit.

The IRS's second computer check also provides for automatic adjustments to the taxpayer's return *before* any audit is made. This "Unallowable Items Program" is designed to catch clearly illegal deductions such as taking your dog as a dependent, claiming an exemption for a spouse who is filing separately, or claiming a partial exemption for half a dependent. Under this program, the computer cross checks your reported income against the W-2 forms from your employer. The dividends and interest reported by banks, brokerage houses, and other financial institutions are also matched against what was listed on the tax return.

Another mistake commonly picked up by this program is a claim for deductions that exceed limits set by the Internal Revenue Code. For example, not all medical and drug expenses may be claimed. You may itemize and write off only those medical expenses that exceed 3 percent of your adjusted gross income, and drug costs beyond 4 percent of your adjusted gross income. The Unallowable Items Program is also likely to catch excessive deductions for charitable contributions, failure to reduce a "casualty loss" by $100 as required by the Internal Revenue Code, and any deduction of interest paid on money borrowed to buy tax-exempt bonds. When an adjustment is made, the taxpayer receives a letter allowing him to explain or protest. If he accepts the change, he is asked to sign the "correction notice."

Unless the mistakes are extensive, these automatic adjustments do not usually lead to a full audit of the taxpayer's return. However, basic errors like these should be avoided. Any time a taxpayer's return is made to stand out, for any reason, it increases his chances for a full audit with its corresponding consequences.

The third Internal Revenue Service program for checking tax returns is the "Questionable Items Program." Here, the taxpayer's whole return, or a specific part of it, is subjected to a detailed investigation: the taxpayer is being challenged rather than corrected. He must justify each and every deduction to the last penny, and to the satisfaction of the examining Internal Revenue Service agent.

IRS computer programs use three techniques to decide which returns to review under this program: random selection, "discriminate function" selection, and special target selection.

The taxpayer's income, claimed deductions, or profession is irrelevant when returns are selected at random. A student earning only $3,000 a year at part-time jobs may be invited to his local Internal Revenue Service office for a tax audit and find himself sitting next to a business executive making $300,000 a year who has also been picked out for audit under this system.

Once the return is in the computer, the taxpayer is at the mercy of the second selection criteria—discriminant function analysis (DIF). Based on previous experience, the Internal Revenue Service has created a number of composite hypothetical "taxpayers." To compute the current DIF averages and weights, the IRS uses a special program called "Taxpayer Compliance and Measurement Program" (TCMP). Based on a random selection of taxpayers, this program establishes the composite norms. Unfortunately, this can be a horror for the taxpayer selected as a "norm." He must answer questions about every single item on his return. He has to produce a birth certificate, marriage certificate, the whole works: every item is checked and the results fed into the computer. In a discriminant function analysis, the characteristics of these "average" taxpayers are given different weights and compared to a return selected for audit.

First, the taxpayer's deductions are added up and weighed for what is called the DIF ("Discriminant Function") score. The computer then recommends audits for all returns with a DIF score above a certain number for a specified income level. The computer is also programmed to notice special deviations. For example, it may recommend an audit if all your deductions turn out to be nicely even rounded numbers. It will also compare your deductions to your job. A man who works as a construction laborer rarely will have a need for a home office deduction. Although he may feel justified, a taxpayer earning $10,000 a year probably should not have a $9,000 itemized deduction for local taxes paid. The computer model match takes into account income level, profession, number of dependents claimed, whether your spouse works, and your address. A Park Avenue zip code with a ghetto-level reported income will immediately signal the discriminant function program to recommend an audit.

The details of the program, of course, are a closely guarded secret. What is known is that the computer compares your deductions to those listed for its composite taxpayer and grades them accordingly. It is not known whether a very high deduction will be offset by a low deduction as each one is weighed and graded differently. A single oversized deduction will probably not flag an immediate audit. For the taxpayer, the name of the game is to match the computer's norm as closely as possible. The chart below reveals average deductions claimed in 1975.

## NATIONAL AVERAGE DEDUCTIONS CLAIMED BASED ON ADJUSTED GROSS INCOME IN THOUSANDS

|  | $9–10 | $10–15 | $15–20 | $20–25 |
|---|---|---|---|---|
| Medical Expenses | $ 833 | $ 570 | $ 506 | $ 439 |
| Taxes | 873 | 1,068 | 1,446 | 1,793 |
| Contributions | 382 | 405 | 469 | 534 |
| Interest | 1,164 | 1,274 | 1,540 | 1,679 |

|  | $25–30 | $30–50 | $50–100 | $100–up |
|---|---|---|---|---|
| Medical Expenses | $ 300 | $ 499 | $ 687 | $ 1,058 |
| Taxes | 2,215 | 2,971 | 5,264 | 13,002 |
| Contributions | 683 | 930 | 2,007 | 10,538 |
| Interest | 1,849 | 2,369 | 3,940 | 10,445 |

The Internal Revenue Service administration expects its management to use employee time productively. Each year, therefore, top IRS administrators will "target" taxpayers in specific professions or with incomes from unusual sources where the highest potential monetary recovery may be found.

For example, dentists, doctors, lawyers, and even accountants all may receive much of their income in cash payments. The Internal Revenue Service believes that this permits them to "forget" to report all of their receipts. The tax agency also believes that the incentive to underreport would be greatly dulled if these professionals knew that as a class they were more likely to be audited. Therefore, as a class, they are more likely to be audited.

The Internal Revenue Service audit manual, *The Policies of the Internal Revenue Service Handbook,* sets as the "primary objective" in selection of tax returns *"the highest possible revenue yield from the examination man hours expended,* and the examination of as many returns as is feasible for the maintenance of a high degree of voluntary taxpayer compliance" [author's italics].

Our federal income tax rates are imposed on a graduated progressive schedule. When a taxpayer earns one dollar more than the top of the previous bracket, a higher percentage of that *additional* dollar will be taken as taxes. Therefore, the more money the taxpayer earns, the higher the potential return is likely to be on time invested by the IRS in the case. If an Internal Revenue Service agent denies a $100 deduction to a taxpayer in the 70 percent bracket, the United States Treasury receives $70, as opposed to only $15 from a taxpayer in the 15 percent bracket.

The Internal Revenue Service has found that returns filed by people who make over $50,000 a year provide fertile grounds for audit reviews. The Internal Revenue Service also watches taxpayers with a second or sideline business,

## TABLE 1

The Percentage of 1975 Returns (by Classification) That
Were Subject to Field or Office Audits

| *Individuals* | *Percent* |
|---|---|
| Nonbusiness | |
| Under $10,000, standard deduction | .69 |
| Under $10,000, itemized deduction | 4.30 |
| $10,000 to $50,000 | 2.46 |
| $50,000 and over | 12.43 |
| Business | |
| Under $10,000 | 2.92 |
| $10,000 to $30,000 | 2.10 |
| $30,000 and over | 7.85 |
| Fiduciary | 1.20 |
| Corporation (based on assets) | |
| Under $50,000 | 3.39 |
| $50,000 to $100,000 | 6.43 |
| $100,000 to $250,000 | 7.92 |
| $250,000 to $500,000 | 14.55 |
| $500,000 to $1,000,000 | 18.92 |
| $1,000,000 to $5,000,000 | 34.06 |
| $5,000,000 to $10,000,000 | 39.45 |
| $10,000,000 to $50,000,000 | 39.58 |
| $50,000,000 to $100,000,000 | 55.35 |
| $100,000,000 and over | 78.79 |
| Estate Taxes | |
| Gross Estate | |
| Under $300,000 | 14.79 |
| $300,000 and over | 62.93 |
| Gift Tax | 4.74 |

those who report hefty capital gain income, and anyone who might be involved in a partnership tax shelter. If the income is there to be sheltered, it may also be there for increased taxes to be assessed. (See Table 1)

In 1975 litigation over Internal Revenue Service determinations, the government usually came out ahead:

|  | Taxpayer Won | Compromise | Government Won |
|---|---|---|---|
| Tax Court |  |  |  |
| Small Cases | 10.4% | 27.0% | 62.6% |
| Regular Cases | 12.2% | 34.9% | 52.9% |
| District Court | 22.8% | 15.1% | 62.1% |
| Court of Claims | 30.4% | 23.9% | 45.7% |

There is a fourth reason a taxpayer's return might be chosen for audit. While the Internal Revenue Service does not encourage tax informers through general public appeals, IRS representatives admit that many investigations could not be successfully conducted except through the use of paid informants or the direct purchase of evidence. Most informers are former employees of a business which has been underreporting its income. If the disgruntled employee does not go after the business itself, he may go after its owner, or the manager who dismissed him.

But a neighbor who objects to your loud stereo at midnight or becomes jealous of your new car each year on a reported salary of $8,000, may just as quickly turn informer. These unofficial Internal Revenue Service agents are used extensively where the taxpayer under investigation is engaged in an allegedly illegal activity. Tax informers are normally rewarded with 10 percent of the additional tax collected. To them, though, the money is often secondary to vindictiveness and revenge. So you should keep two rules in mind:

1. Never cheat on your income taxes.
2. If you do "cheat," never anger anyone who might know about it.

A comment should be made about time limits and the statute of limitations. A taxpayer's tax liability is not officially determined until his return has been examined. The law generally gives the Internal Revenue Service three years after the return is filed to assess any additional tax. There are, however, two very important exceptions to this rule. If anyone required to file a return fails to do so, or if he files a false or fraudulent return with intent to evade taxation, the tax may be assessed, or a court proceeding for collection of the tax may be begun *without* assessment, at *any* time! Furthermore, if a taxpayer omits more than 25 percent of his reported gross income from his return, the Internal Revenue Service has six years in which to assess the additional tax. Normally, though, official Internal Revenue Service administrative policy is to initiate an audit within twenty months after the filing date (usually April 15).

Though IRS audit agents are supposed to be impartial, news reports have charged that agency procedures make real impartiality impossible. One auditor said that when the IRS taught him how to review claimed tax deductions, "Our instructors always said, 'When in doubt, throw it out.'"

Once a tax has been assessed, the IRS Collection Division, an army of 6,000 revenue officers, has the responsibility of getting the money. They are not universally loved. According to a Midwestern tax lawyer who has been dealing with the IRS for 15 years:

They are the most highhanded, obnoxious bastards I've ever dealt with. They are almost brutal in their approach. They seem to relish their power, and generally they bully the general citizenry. I don't like them, and I don't know anyone in the (legal) practice who does.

The director of the IRS Collection Division has admitted that allegations of heavy-handed administrative actions and directives are "not unwarranted criticism." In 1974, responding to this criticism, the Collection Division began a complete reappraisal of many of its practices.

This project, called the "Collection Initiative," was intended to ensure that the Collection Division was administering the law "fairly and impartially, that civil tax laws were not being used punitively, and that the Division was using only the level of enforcement needed to accomplish our overall mission."

Despite these professed goals, the director still acknowledges that some Internal Revenue Service employees continue to conduct their audits under an assumption that the average taxpayer will be evasive, unwilling to cooperate, and negligent about his financial affairs.

Many audit agents blame Congress for the public's low opinion of Internal Revenue Service employees. One agent commented, "There are many areas which are called gray areas due to poor writing of the laws by Congress. There has to be flexibility in some areas to account for unusual circumstances. In some specific areas . . . you can get different results if audited in different district offices or if audited by two different agents due to poor regulations."

Almost 90 percent of the agents I interviewed believed that the tax laws allow extensive flexibility in administrative interpretation. As one agent put it, "There seems to be little black and white." These variations can confuse and anger the taxpayer, but rather than blame Congress, which is the true culprit, the taxpayer is likely to blame the Internal Revenue Service. Because the agency is out in the open, because it is tangible, because the taxpayer whose return is being audited can see the Internal Revenue Service agent whose personal interpretation and application of the vague and ambiguous tax law is taking money from his pocket, that taxpayer makes that agent and the Internal Revenue Service the target of his hostilities.

The official IRS audit manual states:

The purpose of an audit is to verify the accuracy of the tax by verifying the information used in arriving at the tax. The Internal Revenue Service is obligated by law to determine and collect from each taxpayer *only* the correct amount of tax due. As a result, Internal Revenue Service employees *must* maintain an impartial view [author's italics].

The audit policy described in that manual should be made a practice, through effective legislation and administration.

# 3/ "PEOPLE DON'T TRUST US." HOW IRS AGENTS DO THEIR JOBS

I remember my first audit. It was hot—the temperature was in the high nineties—and the air was heavy and so humid that if it had begun to rain I couldn't have gotten any wetter. And of course the Internal Revenue Service office wasn't air-conditioned. Between the heat, the humidity, and the feeling of fear that permeated the crowded waiting room, I felt as if I had crawled under a baby's dirty diaper. I had invested almost a decade of my own life training for this moment. I felt almost like one of King Arthur's knights of old, sent out to do battle with the fearsome Internal Revenue Service dragon.

I was representing a teacher who was being challenged on a home office deduction. The auditor disallowed it totally, asserting that "expenses for an office at home were only allowable to college professors" whereas my client was a high school teacher. The auditor was completely wrong. When I supported my claim with a tax court decision the auditor confessed his misunderstanding of the facts. On my way out I wondered how many innocent taxpayers had lost allowable deductions because they failed to bring a lawyer who could refute an agent's "misunderstanding."

Most Internal Revenue Service office audit agents don't work under the best conditions. Unlike the executive administrators in their temperature-controlled carpeted hide-a-ways, most office agents work in what may charitably be called bullpens. Often sharing desks, always appearing secure behind a veil of so-called governmental infallibility, these auditors had the power of fiscal life or death over my clients.

In truth, though, who really were these creatures sitting ominously with pencils poised, ready to burst the tender balloon of my clients' financial stability? Were they in fact government dragons assigned to destroy the fiscal sustenance of American taxpayers, or were they something else, perhaps nothing more than professional bureaucrats, themselves doing little more than complying with rules according to established procedure?

In the summer of 1977, I directed a study of one hundred Internal Revenue Service agents. Despite complaints, the agents interviewed were quick to defend their employer from external media criticism. "I feel that all these attacks have hindered the system," said one. "The country needs funds to run. All taxpayers should pay their way. I feel you as a citizen of the United States should not be concerned about information obtained or the way it is obtained." Other agents reiterated this view. "I feel that most attacks are off base. The Internal Revenue Service bends over backwards to help and work with taxpayers. The Internal Revenue Service is now only involved with taxes and I do not feel that allowing anyone to hide behind the Privacy Act to avoid paying taxes is correct." "Most attacks are unfounded," added another agent. "We are a convenient patsy boy since most people—especially those of low economic status and little education—have been educated to the belief that we are after them. Actually those people get the greatest benefit out of our service."

More than half the agents interviewed felt the public perceives and reacts to their occupation in a negative way. "Their initial reaction is usually one of apprehension and then of contempt," according to one. "Strangers react poorly, they are inhibited and it is hard to break down the barrier," commented another. "Most people react defensively," reported one agent. "Their typical reaction is 'Oh God! One of them!' "

The Internal Revenue Service agents interviewed tried to demonstrate their honesty and integrity. "At all times we try to protect the taxpayer's rights," one declared. "We are as honest as priests," said another; "we're both in the collection business except their boss is more forgiving of mistakes." Agents were also sensitive about allegations that the Internal Revenue Service had been used for political purposes. "I feel very embarrassed by the revelation that the Internal Revenue Service was being used. I try to approach my job professionally and when the Internal Revenue Service is used it becomes difficult to have the public accept the fact that you were not involved with those acts," said another. One agent's response came from the gut: "I get sick."

The agents objected vehemently to allegations of monetary quotas. "No! There are no quotas," declared one. "Quotas in the Internal Revenue Service were eliminated over three years ago," said another. "The Internal Revenue Service cannot keep production information and cannot use any such information in evaluations. As a result, pressure is not involved." "There are no quotas but there is pressure to complete audit cases within a certain time frame," added another agent. "An assigned case should be submitted within three months. If a case isn't completed within that time, we submit a form explaining the circumstances that are holding up completion. There is seldom any pressure beyond providing the explanation."

Other agents said they saw a different kind of pressure. Daily records are kept on the taxpayers audited, the type of case, and the result of the audit contact. Though Internal Revenue Service policy states that it is irrelevant whether an audit results in an adjustment, one agent said, "If the results come out of the computer and say 35 percent of the audits are no change, the pressure from upstairs starts on your supervisor who in turn puts the pressure on the lowly auditor. So you go into an audit and make just the littlest change like adjusting depreciation, or, if it is a question of travel and entertainment, you compromise."

A former Internal Revenue Service field agent explained the old quota system. "There was an unspoken law which said he 'has to get the tax.' Fifteen years ago the quota system for a grade 9 agent was $500 per man day plus 1.2 cases per man day and for grade 11 it was $1,000 per man day and 9 cases per man day. Basically, an agent brought in approximately $100,000 each year but got paid $9,000. Today the quota system doesn't exist. Instead they have what they call Proper Utilization of Time. Promotions are based on PUT but if you spend three days on a no-change case you are not utilizing your time properly." This ex-agent thought PUT was "self defeating." "How," he asked, "are you supposed to analyze a case if they don't recognize that the proper amount of time is needed? This puts the agent under a lot of internal pressure."

How qualified is the average Internal Revenue Service auditor when he sits down to review your return? Most complaints received by the Committee on Tax Administration of the American Institute of Certified Public Accountants can be traced to the lack of training given the office auditors. Of the agents in my study, 86 percent considered the formal Internal Revenue Service training program "adequate." However, 42 percent of this group believed additional formal training should be given annually to help employees "keep up with the latest developments in the tax law."

Among those who felt the training was *not* adequate, the major complaint was that it was "too much at once" to be absorbed well. One agent commented, "It fell short in a couple of areas, especially in the experience with actual books and records. The material used in the audit training did not prepare me sufficiently when I encountered my first set of books."

To perform his job in a fully competent manner, the tax auditor needs to understand the law itself, the Internal Revenue Service publications which interpret that law, and the detailed administrative procedures designed to carry it out. To give its employees this knowledge, the Internal Revenue Service runs an intensive classroom and on-the-job training program. After ten days of on-the-job orientation, the training is provided in three units. The first two units, which together give the new employee 40 days of classroom instruction and 60 days of on-the-job training, are completed within three months of recruitment. The third unit, given only after the trainee demonstrates ability and completes at least six semester hours of accounting courses, consists of 13 days in the classroom and 10 days of on-the-job training.

The first two units cover Internal Revenue Service history, return processing, audit technique, and the law for individual tax returns. Unit three covers taxes for proprietorships, partnerships, estates, and corporations. An advanced training course is also offered for field agents whose audit work for larger corporations involves more complex technical issues. Agents who work in areas outside the regular audit program can receive specialized training in excise taxes, employment taxes, or pension and retirement plans. Additional training is available for changes and updates in the tax law.

The instructor/trainee ratio during unit I is one to five and during unit II, one to six. This permits very close supervision, including instructor participation in audits and review of cases. The Internal Revenue Service does recognize, though, that during on-the-job training the inexperience of a new tax auditor may adversely affect the quality of an audit. Clearly, if an auditor with no tax or accounting background beyond ten days of preclassroom orientation reviews a return, he cannot be expected to perform as complete or as competent an evaluation as could an auditor with ten years of practical experience. The taxpayer whose return is being reviewed should be aware of this, and respond accordingly. If an agent quotes a rule of tax law with which you are not familiar you might politely ask him to show you the written source. You can say it's for your records.

The Internal Revenue Service's training program was evaluated by the American Council on Education in March 1975. The council was so impressed with the quality of the progam that it advised colleges and universities to grant up to six upper division credit hours to Internal Revenue Service employees who successfully complete the training program and later pursue a masters degree in tax law. This represents one quarter of the credits normally required for the full degree.

The average taxpayer is likely to come in contact with four types of Internal Revenue Service employees: the office auditor, the field agent, the collection agent, and the intelligence agent.

According to one agent, at one time in order to be hired as an office auditor, the entry level position, an applicant need not have a college degree, though he must have taken the civil service test. He then had to take and pass the government's office audit test. If he cleared that hurdle, he had to pass one more written exam before his name was placed on the "registrar's list." Finally, he was put before a board for a strenuous interview and examination. His own tax returns for the last three years were audited and his background checked. Today he still does not need a college degree but need pass only the civil service exam (the Professional Administration Career Exam) and complete 6 credits in accounting within his first two years on the job.

If the applicant survives the above "ordeal" he becomes an office auditor. His main job is to review and verify the tax returns of individuals, usually wage earners. He performs this audit within the Internal Revenue Service office itself, rather than at the home or business of the individual taxpayer. Therefore, his review power and the scope of the returns he audits are limited by the physical and practical ability of the taxpayer to transport his records to the Internal Revenue Service office. The individual proprietor who owns and operates a local discount shop, for example, would rarely be subject to an office audit. The records of most value in an audit of this taxpayer would most easily and conveniently be found at the individual's home or office, so he would probably face a "field audit" instead.

The field agent examines not only the more sophisticated individual returns, but those of partnerships and corporations as well. While he may call his "cases" into the Internal Revenue Service Office, his normal procedure is to go where the records can be found—at the taxpayer's home or business.

To qualify for this more rigorous assignment, the field agent must have a college degree. Furthermore, he must have accumulated 24 credits in accounting. In his job he must work with professionals on a professional basis.

If the office auditor or field agent determines that a tax

deficiency is due, but it is not forthcoming, the taxpayer is soon greeted by the collection agent. The mission of the Internal Revenue Service Collection Division historically has been to "encourage and achieve the highest degree of voluntary compliance with the filing and paying requirements of the Internal Revenue laws," according to Division Director Thomas L. Davis. He said the division collects unpaid accounts, determines and analyzes why taxpayers become delinquent and, through various means, tries to prevent taxpayers' accounts from becoming delinquent in the future. In short, the collection agent's job is to get the money the Internal Revenue Service believes is due. Quite often, he becomes adept at drawing blood out of a stone. His tools range from a polite letter or phone call, a personal visit to your home or business, to the often heavy-handed levy and seizure actions known as jeopardy or termination assessments (see chapter 1).

The fourth type of Internal Revenue Service employee the taxpayer might encounter is the intelligence agent. His appearance on your doorstep mandates a closed mouth and an immediate call to your lawyer. The Intelligence Division is responsible for the enforcement of the criminal provisions of the tax laws. These agents investigate evasion of income, estate, gift, and excise taxes and failure to file returns. The filing of false statements, false claims for refunds, and the preparation of false returns for others also fall in this agent's domain. When evidence of tax evasion or tax fraud is found, intelligence agents investigate and can recommend criminal prosecution.

Recent special intelligence investigations have focused on tax evasion by large corporations, the abuse of foreign tax havens, corruption of public officials through payoffs and kickbacks, and the preparation of fraudulent tax returns. In 1976, the Intelligence Division completed 8,797 investigations and recommended prosecution of 3,147 taxpayers. Prosecution and trial were completed in 1,193 cases; 1,172 taxpayers received federal prison

IRS intelligence agents are efficient, sophistic
very effective. In California they uncovered an
scheme in which 15 individuals filed 357 fictitio
in an attempt to obtain over $743,748 in refund
Jersey, a businessman was sentenced to 18 months in jail
and fined $35,000 for signing corporate and individual in-
come tax returns he knew were false. Additional taxes and
penalties in that case exceeded $1.5 million.

In Memphis, an osteopathic physician was subjected to
a "net worth" investigation. In such a study, the Internal
Revenue Service compares the taxpayer's style of life to
the amount of income reported. For example, someone
reporting only $12,000 in income would have a lot of hard
explaining to do if he drove a $20,000 car and lived in a
$200,000 mansion. The Memphis physician was convicted
of evading over $83,000 in taxes and is now behind bars,
thanks to the intelligence agents of the Internal Revenue
Service.

To most agents I interviewed, the main attraction of an
IRS career is the total job security it offers. One agent ob-
served, "There has never been a reduction in force in the
Internal Revenue Service, so if stability is something you'd
look for, this is it." "The demands are reasonable; if a job
is done to meet reasonable standards, a job is secure for-
ever," another agent said. "Total job security," declared
another.

"It is impossible to be fired, no matter how incompetent
you are. If management really wants to get rid of you, they
will certify that you have an emotional disorder caused by
the job and give you a disability pension even if there is
nothing wrong."

Another agent responded, "I feel quite secure and feel
confident in making long range plans based on continuing
salary. In public accounting or in industry, one cannot say
that. Unfortunately, Internal Revenue Service security is

like teacher tenure and people who aren't doing an adequate job are kept on."

In short, as one angry agent put it, "You really can't get fired unless you're grossly incompetent or take a bribe."

Security was not the only reason for staying with the Internal Revenue Service. "Stable hours," a "great deal of freedom," "challenge and good benefits" were all given as advantages of government employment. Most agents found working for the Internal Revenue Service not only "interesting and pleasant," but "satisfying and "emotionally gratifying" as well. Eight out of ten field agents were happy with their work. "Each day I go to a different business, no routine. I set my own appointments and schedule my work myself," said one.

Many were proud of the professional nature of their jobs. "I am able to work as a professional," declared one agent. Another commented, "I enjoy the work. I enjoy researching law and I get into it quite heavily most of the time. It's also a professional position with a lot of responsibility." One agent revealed a quiet satisfaction in being able to "make a contribution to keeping America together."

Many agents said they liked the fixed working hours and limited supervision. "It's a 9 to 5 job," said one. "When I leave the office I forget my work." Almost 70 percent of the agents agreed that there was very little supervision. "We take on a great deal of responsibility," one agent said. "If a problem does arise, we are usually in contact with the supervisor to get his opinion. The supervisor cannot do our audits for us; he can only recommend but not force us to change our position on an issue." Another agent commented that "Supervision is on a problem solving basis. Our supervisor is there to help when the problem cannot be solved at our level. The supervisor provides each agent with current policies and tax law updates."

At first, advancement in the agency is based on time served. Four early salary increases are automatic. But once an employee reaches a journeyman's level, increases are based on skill evaluation, or at least are supposed to be. Several agents expressed their doubts. "The degree of objectivity used by supervisors leaves something to be desired," one agent commented. Another complained, "Subjective evaluations with promotions are generally given to those well-liked by supervisors and are not based primarily on performance." A third agent explained the promotion policy in his office in simple terms: "The number of butts you lick will normally determine the extent of your advance."

Many of these agents did not foresee a permanent career with the Internal Revenue Service. Two were straightforward in explaining their present employment. "It was the best I could find," said one. Another said he chose the Internal Revenue Service "because I like to eat." A third agent was following a timetable: "I do my work to the best of my ability and I get paid for it. There is little satisfaction here, though, and I will probably be leaving in the next two to three years."

The quality of working conditions varied from office to office. Agents bewailed "army reject" desks, lack of space, and government cost-cutting measures: "They took our desks away and gave us ordinary tables to work on. This stinks to say the least. The office I'm in is too overcrowded," one agent lamented. Field agents, though, spend 90 percent of their work hours away from their office. Their working conditions vary with the cases they audit and for one agent ranged from "a chairman's couch in a corporate board room to a cardboard box in the back room of a gas station."

Reports from other agents were not as encouraging about either Internal Revenue Service supervision or hours actually worked. "Field auditors like myself work from 9:30 to 4:00 and we get taken out to lunch a lot," reported one. When he works at the Internal Revenue Service home office his routine is somewhat different. "I spend as much time on a case as I need, and on a typical day at the home office I do three hours of hard work and then coast and bullshit the rest of the day."

While direct supervision for experienced agents is minimal, the omnipresent eye of administrative scrutiny is often felt. One agent feared that his phone was sporadically "bugged" to check his honesty. Another revealed, "I tend to get paranoid at times. Our work is constantly checked and our moral character is constantly scrutinized. This gets to me at times."

More than a third of the agents questioned in my study complained about IRS administrators in emotion-laden and very frank terms. One said, "Management tends to be too concerned with the statistics and numbers game. The forms we have to complete each month are a drag." "The lack of common sense on their part can be very discouraging," said another.

A third agent was brutal in his evaluation of the Internal Revenue Service administration in his office: "It is very disheartening and a pain in the butt. Apparently, the Peter Principle applied here," he declared.

He was not alone. "All procedures and duties are outlined in the manual," an agent declared. "The manual can be defined as a procedural guide that promotes inefficiency, waste, red tape, unnecessary paper work, and a bungling bureaucracy. In short, administration is a mess!"

An agent interviewed in another study concurred, "At least 50 percent of all of the supervisors stink. . . . Shit really rises to the top."

Of the one in five agents who were dissatisfied with their job, most complained of a lack of purpose. "It's like working 8:00 to 4:30, five days a week, and never accomplishing anything," said one. Another cried, "I can't claim that I make a contribution to society, so there is no satisfaction in that area."

Compensation and performance evaluation were two

areas on which the agents held strong opinions. Thirty-two percent were clearly dissatisfied with their salary. According to one agent, "The lack of collective bargaining rules has resulted in Internal Revenue salaries falling 20 percent below the market in the last ten years. For example, private wages often rose 5 percent per year. In dollars, I could increase my pay by 30 percent by leaving to go to private industry." Perhaps the security and satisfaction this employee found at the IRS outweighed his monetary concerns. Of the 68 percent who were satisfied, almost 40 percent thought they should receive more money. Half of those who were financially content had been with the Internal Revenue Service for six years or more—they were tenured agents.

Despite some pride in their profession, almost half the agents I surveyed said they were hesitant to reveal their occupation to people they meet. "I don't broadcast it," said one, "but I answer straightforwardly when asked." Others said they refer to themselves as "government employees" or "accountants" when asked by people they meet for the first time. Among the 14 percent of the agents who did keep their position quiet, most were veteran Internal Revenue Service employees. Their general feeling was: "People don't trust us."

If honest taxpayers help make our voluntary system of taxation work, an equally important element is honest tax collectors. In fact, the one characteristic most essential in an Internal Revenue Service employee is honesty. The agency is paranoid about any allegations or even insinuations concerning employee bribe-taking, and the Internal Revenue Service as a whole is probably one of our most honest governmental agencies. Yet the temptations there are greatest, the opportunities most available. Some agents yield to them.

For example, Internal Revenue Service Supervisor Cyril J. Niederberger was convicted in Pittsburgh of illegally accepting gratuities from Gulf Oil Corporation when his office was investigating alleged illegal campaign contributions made by that company. U.S. District Court Judge Daniel Snider placed Niederberger on five years probation and fined him $5,000 for accepting paid vacations in Florida, Nevada, California, and New Jersey. Gulf had allegedly paid expenses totaling $3,294.92 for Niederberger, including:

A hotel bill for $306.80 at the Beachcomber Lodge and Villas, Pompano Beach, Florida, in July 1971.

Round-trip fare to Miami, plus meals and lodging at the Doral Country Club totaling $445.16 in January 1973.

Round-trip air fare to Absecon, New Hampshire, plus meals and lodging at the Seaview Country Club, totaling $664.71 in August 1973.

Round-trip air fare to Pebble Beach, California, plus meals and lodging at the Del Monte Lodge worth $690.93 in April 1974.

Round-trip air fare to Las Vegas, plus meals and lodging at the Desert Inn, totaling $1,187.32 in June 1974.

To keep an eye on its agents, the IRS has established an Internal Security Division (ISD). This secret police force investigates complaints of criminal and noncriminal misconduct and irregularities concerning IRS employees. It also investigates persons outside the Internal Revenue Service who are suspected of trying to bribe or otherwise corrupt service employees, or who threaten or assault employees. Internal Security Division inspectors also conduct background checks on Internal Revenue Service job applicants. (Table 2)

In 1976, the Internal Security Division was responsible for the arrest or indictment of 125 individuals, including 27 IRS employees or former employees and 98 taxpayers or tax practitioners. A total of 90 defendants were convicted during the year, including 71 who pleaded guilty rather than go to trial. Forty-three of these convictions were for bribery, 27 were for assault, and the rest involved such other criminal actions as embezzlement, conspiracy to defraud the government, and obstruction of justice.

The most direct challenge to Internal Revenue Service integrity is through attempted bribery. In 1976, the Internal Revenue Inspection Service, a branch of the Security Divi- Revenue Inspection Service, a branch of the Accounts, Collections, and Taxpayer Service Division, investigated 204 possible bribery attempts, resulting in 51 arrests or indictments. Between fiscal year 1962, when the Inspection Service was placed in charge of bribery investigations, and July 1976, agents investigated 1,851 alleged bribery attempts. These investigations led to 493 arrests or indictments and 372 convictions or guilty pleas. The other cases failed for lack of evidence.

Successful investigations resulted in disaster for both taxpayers and employees who attempted to cheat the federal treasury. Evidence gathered by the IRS forced a New Jersey CPA and his client to plead guilty to bribery and conspiracy when they were charged with paying a revenue agent $3,500 for a favorable audit. The judge fined the accountant $20,000, ordered his license revoked, and prohibited him from preparing tax returns for his clients in the future. The client received a two-year suspended sentence and a $20,000 fine.

In another case, two Las Vegas casino operators and a businessman were arrested after making bribery payments totaling $64,000 to improperly influence civil and criminal investigations. In Hawaii, four Honolulu jade importers

## TABLE 2

### Internal Security Division Investigations

| Type of Investigations and Actions | 1974 | 1975 | 1976 |
|---|---|---|---|
| Total Investigations | 21,322 | 18,265 | 17,004 |
| Personnel Investigations | | | |
| Character and Security | 13,823 | 11,104 | 10,291 |
| Conduct | 1,367 | 1,063 | 1,011 |
| Special Inquiries | 2,711 | 2,561 | 2,503 |
| Total Personnel Investigations | 17,901 | 14,728 | 13,805 |
| Total Other Investigations | 3,421 | 3,537 | 3,199 |
| *Actions by Management Officials on Personnel Investigations* | | | |
| Total Actions | 17,901 | 14,728 | 13,805 |
| [1]Separations | 331 | 256 | 237 |
| Suspensions from Duty and Pay | 115 | 74 | 87 |
| Reprimands, Warnings, and Demotions | 1,033 | 796 | 633 |
| Rejected for Employment | 329 | 195 | 199 |
| Pending Adjudication | — | — | 502 |
| [2]Non-Disciplinary Actions | 16,093 | 13,407 | 12,147 |
| *Separations by Type of Offense* | | | |
| Bribery, Extortion, or Collusion | 2 | 5 | 6 |
| Embezzlement or Theft of Funds or Property | 3 | 8 | 11 |
| Failure of Employee to Pay Proper Tax | 66 | 23 | 21 |
| Falsification or Distortion of Reports, Records, etc. | 117 | 123 | 105 |
| Unauthorized Outside Activity | 3 | 2 | 4 |
| Failure to Discharge Duties Properly | 10 | 12 | 6 |

TABLE 2 (con't)

| | | | |
|---|---|---|---|
| Divulgence of Confidential Information | 2 | 4 | 6 |
| Acceptance of Fees and Gratuities | 2 | 4 | 2 |
| Refusal to Cooperate in Official Investigation | 1 | 0 | 2 |
| Personal and Other Misconduct | 125 | 75 | 74 |
| Total Separations | 331 | 256 | 237 |

1. Includes resignations, retirements, or other separations while employees were under investigation or before administrative decision was made on disciplinary action where investigation disclosed derogatory information.
2. Includes clearance and closed without action letters on conduct investigations.

and gold jewelry dealers were indicted after they tried to pay a revenue agent and a customs agent a total of nearly $10,000 to overlook or reduce their tax liabilities.

In 1976, a California massage parlor and health spa owner was arrested on charges of attempting to pay a revenue agent $500 for a no-change audit on the spa's 1973, 1974, and 1975 tax returns. The same year, a New York taxpayer was indicted for offering a revenue agent a $5,000 bribe in return for favorable audits of his individual tax return and a corporate return in which the taxpayer was a major stockholder.

Investigators were very busy in New York in 1976. A New York accountant pleaded guilty to conspiracy to bribe a revenue agent after he paid the agent $2,000 to reduce a proposed corporate tax liability from $30,000 to $253. In addition, a CPA from New York pleaded guilty to bribery charges after he paid $3,500 to a revenue agent for a favorable audit of a client: $450 to a District Office auditor for a favorable audit of another client: and an additional $125 to the agent in the first case to help fix the second case.

Statistics regarding the Internal Security Division's investigations of Internal Revenue Service show that IRS employees who engage in improper or illegal behavior constitute a very small percentage of the workforce. Most investigations of alleged impropriety led to exoneration of the employees involved. Given the potential for fiscal enticement, this is a record to be admired.

Agents quoted in this chapter made their comments in interviews with law students who were conducting a study of the IRS under my supervision. The project was authorized and coordinated through the IRS Office of Public Relations. The agents responding were promised that they would not be identified. Two proposed questions were never asked, on orders from the Internal Revenue Service administration. The first was "What is the impact of changes in the Internal Revenue Service administration—e.g. a commissioner change? Do you personally feel this impact?" The second question, which almost led to the complete cancellation of the project, was "How are policy changes made by political appointees effectuated on the local level? Explain." One might wonder why, in a free society, a government agency which is supposed to represent the American people, which asks us to reveal to them our innermost financial secrets, forbade these two questions. Perhaps the lack of public trust, about which long-term IRS agents complain, results from the lack of honest openness on the part of the Internal Revenue Service bureaucracy.

In the spring of 1977, Cornelius J. Coleman was appointed District Director for the Internal Revenue Service in New Jersey. Responsible for 1,800 workers in 14 offices overseeing the filing of 4.7 million individual, corporate, and other returns representing over $10.8 billion in federal tax money, Coleman came to his new job concerned about the tax agency's image as an "oppressive ogre" to many segments of the public.

"We want to impress on the people that the Internal Revenue Service is not out to harass the taxpayer. We're here to provide service and assistance in helping them discharge their responsibilities under the tax law," he explained. "Our mission is a simple one. It's to promote compliance with that law on a voluntary basis. We intend to promote the most efficient, effective, and courteous service available to help make the law, and the people's responsibilities under it, easier to understand."

To accomplish this, Coleman promised to "strip away some of the mystique" which has obscured the public's image of the tax agency. Taking him at his word, in the fall of 1977 I sought to expose my class of tax law students to the fact that Internal Revenue Service employees were just "people," not fearsome "ogres." I therefore assigned them individually or in groups to interview any Internal Revenue Service employee and ask questions such as: "What do you do?" "How do you do it?" "Why do you work for the IRS?" "Do you enjoy it?" "How does the IRS function administratively?" "How is an agent trained?" "How is a return selected for audit?" These were not to be "authorized" interviews controlled or directed by the Internal Revenue Service. While promising confidentiality, I asked my students to identify to me the employee interviewed.

The response was shocking, even to me. For three weeks my telephones, both at home and in my office, were constantly ringing. The callers were IRS employees who asked me, usually very politely, to call off the study and get my students out of their offices. These people told me that they were too busy, that they couldn't be bothered, that the study was disruptive, that they didn't have the time to help. Some of the employees who called me seemed to be both harried and very scared.

The Internal Revenue *Service* is supposed to be a service. What better service could they provide than giving fifteen minutes of their time to help educate a tax law student as to the role of an Internal Revenue Service employee? What better way to "strip away the mystique," to quash the "ogre"

image, as Director Coleman had put it? Instead of cooperation, my students were told that these interviews were impossible, that they were clearly against Internal Revenue
Service policy, and therefore strictly prohibited. On September 12, 1977, Public Information Officer Henry Holmes was
cooperative enough to send me a letter plainly pointing out
that these interviews were *not* against Internal Revenue
Service policy but noting that they would be given, if at all,
on a purely voluntary basis.

Mr. Holmes forwarded copies of his letter to all Internal
Revenue Service local offices in the district. It was to be of
little avail. The attitude taken by the Internal Revenue Service personnel was that of an adversary, rather than ally,
of the public. Even when confronted directly by a student
with a copy of the Holmes letter in hand, these "public
servants" consistently responded to questions with "no
comment," "no opinion," or "It's nobody's business." One
student reported feeling that he was "trespassing on holy
ground; that the Internal Revenue Service, although a mere
subsection of the entire Federal government, was rather a
superior body with a different set of principles than other
government agencies and regulatory commissions."

Internal Revenue Service employees were described as
"arrogant," "lazy," "discourteous," and "absorbed in their
own power." Almost universally the students saw them as
having a "paranoid hang-up about the secrecy of their job."

All Internal Revenue Service employees are properly prohibited from disclosing "all returns and return information." But they were not being asked to disclose confidential
information. Questions about employee selection procedure,
training, and adult guidelines can under no stretch of the
imagination be said to relate to "return information." Most
of what was asked either already is or should be public
information. Why certain returns are selected for review or,
at least, the basis for the selection decision is not the type

of information that Congress ever intended to be kept confidential.

Many students were able to find people to interview. Most of them were ex-employees or family friends. Some Internal Revenue Service agents found time after work to meet with my students. They proved that a sense of public responsibility did exist within the Internal Revenue Service. Unfortunately, though, the most pervasive reaction was pure paranoia. While for my class the "ogre" myth was destroyed, in too many cases it was replaced by an image of "frightened puppets."

I was very surprised at the reaction my students received. In my own dealings with Internal Revenue Service employees I have been "misinformed" as to the law on several occasions but have always been treated with courtesy and respect. Of course, an attorney in a three-piece suit with a knowledge of the law presents a different image from a college student in jeans.

Perhaps what we might do is follow the example of the government in Manila. The Philippines Bureau of Internal Revenue has decided its employees must pass a neuropsychiatric test before being promoted. Officials said this was because the duties of tax workers required "honesty, tact, diplomacy, courtesy, and control of temper." Maybe then our own Internal Revenue Service could be found free of "evasion."

# 4/WHY THE IRS KEEPS TAX AUDITS SECRETS

"Publicity is the cure for governmental evils."

Senator William George Norris
U.S. Senate, 1926

Much of the American fear of the Internal Revenue Service derives from its reputation as a secret agency. The IRS has traditionally hidden its activities, its internal administrative policies and management directives, behind a wall of darkness. This withholding of information from the American public creates a climate of taxpayer uncertainty. Few taxpayers can comprehend the intricate complexities of the tax code itself, but when a taxpayer is refused, because "it's policy," even access to the administrative rules of the agency which is to judge the adequacy and honesty of his tax return, he soon develops a fear of the unknown. The tangible symbol of that unknown is the Internal Revenue audit agent.

The Internal Revenue Service has recognized this problem. The agency's Public Information Division is responsible for developing information programs, evaluating public response to those programs, and presenting the "correct" image of the Internal Revenue Service. Much of this division's work involves press releases and consultation with journalists. Almost all of it can be accurately described as public relations.

The agency's image, however, comes not from the Public Information Division efforts, but from the way in which IRS employees do their job. To improve the taxpayer–tax agent relationship, the Internal Revenue Service has invested in massive and unique programs of tax information and assistance. Internal Revenue Service employees will now answer individual and specific tax questions, will send you tax forms with instructions attempting to help you fill them out, and, in most cases, will even fill out the forms for you.

Many of these programs were prompted by the Freedom of Information Act of 1967, which called for disclosure of and public access to material concerning the workings of our government. The Internal Revenue Service's first response to the Act, though, was far from one of voluntary compliance. The agency's tradition of strict internal secrecy was so strong that initially, the Freedom of Information Act led to no relaxation at all in the official IRS rule of silence. No mafioso, swearing blood oaths to the code of *Omerta*, was ever more tight-lipped. Then, in 1969, the Internal Revenue Service decided to challenge the personal and corporate tax returns of Philip and Sue Long of Bellevue, Washington.

After an audit of the Longs' returns for 1966, 1967, and 1968, the IRS assessed $38,144 in addition to the $21,412 already paid. Long was a real estate developer, and the IRS ruled that he could not deduct certain expenditures as business expenses. Long cooperated completely with the government auditors. Whatever materials and information they requested, he quickly furnished. He expected the cooperation to be matched by the IRS. It wasn't.

Long wanted to know how the IRS had arrived at each decision regarding items in his return. The agency ignored or avoided his questions. Long's personal investigations revealed that almost every IRS decision was, in one way or another, "negotiable" with regard to amounts due or rulings applied. Moreover, he found that written IRS guidelines covered the nature and scope of these negotiations, but that only IRS employees could obtain copies.

Long demanded access to these booklets and to documents describing the official taxpayer audit procedures. He also requested access to figures showing how much money and manpower the IRS actually expended in auditing returns.

He was met with a stone wall. The Internal Revenue Service told him that its manuals, handbooks, and reports were "classified" and therefore "unavailable to the public." So he decided to sue to obtain the material. Acting under the Freedom of Information Act of 1967, he demanded copies of "all handbooks and manuals used by the Internal Revenue Service to instruct its agents in their dealings with taxpayers."

Long made several trips to Washington, D.C., interviewed 80 members of Congress, prepared 300 pages of briefs and legal memoranda, and published as ads, at his own expense, eleven articles called *Life under the IRS* in the *Washington Post*. Early in his confrontation with the Internal Revenue Service, Long had been threatened with a jeopardy assessment. But before his property was seized, the publication of his articles in the *Post* made him a public figure, a "sensitive case," and the IRS decided not to use the drastic jeopardy assessment for fear of its impact on the agency's public image.

On August 10, 1972, U.S. District Judge William T. Beeks ruled that it was unlawful for the Internal Revenue Service to withhold its in-house manuals and statistics from the public. The Longs had won, but it had cost them over $10,000 just to get permission to see the rules and guidelines.

Immediately after Judge Beeks ruled in his favor, Long went to the Internal Revenue Service office in Seattle and asked to see the in-house manual called the *Closing Agreement Handbook*. This was the agency's official guide for auditing returns, negotiating settlements, and making final deals with taxpayers.

Public Information Clerk Bernice Landry refused! Long had to call Internal Revenue Service attorney Joseph Greaves into the room personally before he was given the handbook for copying. Even then he had to do it on IRS premises and at a cost of 25 cents per page.

Long was eventually permitted to visit Internal Revenue Service training schools. Here he found that agents "were trained that when they come to audit a taxpayer's return, the presumption is that the taxpayer has cheated and the only question to figure out is how much more he owes the government."

Long's other revelations were just as shocking. He detailed the Internal Revenue Service quota system, euphemistically referred to as "target goals," and exposed the gross statistical disparities in audit settlements. Long also found the Internal Revenue Service desperately sensitive about its public image. He noted that the agency distributed volumes of information on taxpayer arrests, indictments, and convictions, but that IRS defeats were carefully concealed or underplayed. The manual even advised that the auditor settle for little or nothing if the taxpayer seemed ready to go to court and had a good chance of winning the case. The key was the fear that an adverse judicial decision in a case the taxpayer brought to court would become binding precedent. The question of whether the taxpayer's position was legally correct was considered secondary. In 1977, after an eight-year battle with the IRS, the Longs won their tax case. The Ninth Circuit Court upheld their original returns. Long said, "This means we have won on all the issues."

The Long case cracked the wall of silence and secrecy surrounding the Internal Revenue Service. Internal Revenue Service internal manuals are now public and open for all Internal Revenue Service district offices and, on April 1, 1974, the agency established a Disclosure Division to handle all matters arising under the Freedom of Information Act. It would seem, then, that IRS decision-making has come out from behind its shield of secrecy and into the sunshine of public exposure. But has it really?

G. Warren Kearse is an author and a tax protester. Unlike most people, he wants to be audited. As a matter of fact, in 1977 he brought all his records to the Internal Revenue Service Building in Washington, D.C., and asked to be audited. But there was one catch: Kearse wanted an official record of his audit interview. The Internal Revenue Service refused. Kearse was told that the audit interview could not be tape-recorded, nor could an official transcript be kept.

"This could be a violation of privacy," one employee said.

"That act is to protect me, not you," he replied. Kearse offered to give up any rights to privacy which he might have had in return for an "accurate record" of what might happen at the audit interview.

Kearse refused to turn off his own tape recorder unless the Internal Revenue Service promised to give him an authorized recording of the proceedings.

"That's impossible," shouted Kenneth J. Wood of the Internal Revenue Service. "We don't keep records of these audits."

Kearse asked if there was a law prohibiting a transcript. Wood couldn't cite one. "It's policy," he said.

Kearse refused to be audited without an official transcript of the proceedings. Upset, Wood had no recourse.

"That's it. The interview is over," he said. Wood turned and left the room. As he reached the door he looked back at Kearse. "You can go," he snapped.

To get permission to record an Internal Revenue Service audit interview, a written request must be sent to the Internal Revenue Service district director. Permission is not always given. If the people being audited agree to making the recording, it is hard to see why the Internal Revenue Service would object. What would the IRS want to keep hidden? Obviously, the cult of secrecy still exists in the Internal Revenue Service.

In one form or another, secrecy has been an issue in federal income tax administration since Congress passed the first income tax in July, 1862, to help pay for the civil war debt. The tax act required that all income tax returns be published in at least four public places and for at least 15 days. Congress believed that if each taxpayer knew exactly how much his neighbor paid, everyone would be kept honest.

The battle for tax return confidentiality began immediately. In 1864, disclosure of "the operations, style of work, or apparatus of any manufacturer or producer" was prohibited. An Internal Revenue Service employee who divulged such information was subject to a fine of $1,000, one year in prison, and, of course, "dismissal from duty." On July 4, 1870, Congress passed legislation which prohibited publication of any private material submitted to the Internal Revenue Service. Specifically, the act said in part:

... no collector, deputy collector, assessor or assistant assessor shall permit to be published in any manner such income returns or any part thereof, except such general statistics not

specifying names of individuals as be made public under rules
and regulations as the Commissioner of the Internal Revenue
shall prescribe.

The confidentiality debate was not over, though. Interest-
ingly, it centered not on the disclosure of individual tax
returns but rather on the release of corporate returns. Both
Presidents William Howard Taft and Teddy Roosevelt argued for disclosure. Taft argued, "If now by a perfectly
legitimate and effective system of taxation, we are inciden-
tally able to possess the Government and the stockholders
and the public of the knowledge of real business transactions . . . of every corporation in the country we have made a
long step toward that supervisory control which may prevent a further abuse of power."

Roosevelt agreed. "The first requisite is knowledge, full
and complete—knowledge which may be made public to the
world. . . . Publicity can do no harm to the honest corporation, and we need not be overtender with sparing the dishonest corporation."

Taft and Roosevelt were not without opposition in Congress. Senator William Hughes of New Jersey said, "I
propose to vote against giving the President, or any administrative or executive officer the right to publish facts as
against any particular corporation around election time and
not publish facts as regards to other corporations. . . ."

Senator Oscar Wilder Underwood of Alabama stated similar views: "I think the greatest folly that has ever been put
on the statute book of this country is this law to make every
little crossroads corporation report publicly. . . ."

The question was resolved with the fine legal reasoning
that was to become the foundation of our tax system. The
returns themselves were not to be subject to public inspection. But these same returns were to become public records
and therefore open to inspection as such!

Corporations are public entities, created by the law. The

law, therefore, may correctly demand full and complete disclosure of corporate tax returns. Individual returns, on the other hand, require more protection. Debate on the privacy of individual tax returns began when the Supreme Court ruled in the Treasury Decisions of 1914 that "returns of individuals shall not be subject to inspection by any one except the proper officers and employees of the Treasury Department."

In 1916, Senator Paul Oscar Husting of Wisconsin argued for increased disclosure. "I think it is quite difficult to give any sound reason why these records should not be public, and, furthermore, I can not see why if corporations . . . are subject to having the returns examined, the individual should not have his income tax return made public, or at least subject to examination."

The senator proposed an admendment to simplify the processing of tax returns and to make those returns public. He argued that his measure would help stop the income tax evasion of that time.

Senator Husting believed that tax evasion put an unreasonable burden on the honest taxpayer. "Yet you make it easy by putting the cloak over the tax returns, for the situation to exist whereby one man who has a conscience . . . and is honest must pay his share of income tax and his neighbor can escape under the seal of secrecy. . . . He [the honest man] has an interest in that money that is paid as taxes by his neighbor, because in so far as his neighbor . . . escapes his share of taxes it is piled on him."

The Senate rejected Husting's amendment, apparently fearing, as did Senator Sinclair Weeks of Massachusetts, that it would "make every man a detective to spy on the actions of his neighbors."

Each time a new revenue act was proposed, the battle over tax confidentiality began anew. The proponents of disclosure argued for the people's right to know and declared that taxpayers would be more honest if they knew their returns would be open to public inspection. More income tax would therefore be collected. "If a man has made an honest return, how can his feelings be injured even then, if that mistake is corrected and made right—whichever way it may be?"

The opposition feared that citizens would not report their true income if it were to be made public, for fear of robbery. Their major argument, however, was that people have a right to privacy concerning their business affairs, a right they believed had been granted early in American history.

In 1924 the commissioner of the Internal Revenue Service was required to publish a list showing each person making a return, his address, and the amount of tax paid. After a year of this publicity, the Treasury Department voiced its opposition and recommended repeal:

The publicity is utterly useless from a Treasury standpoint. . . . All of the supervising Internal Revenue agents report that no additional tax has been collected due to the publicity provision, and all of them recommend its repeal. There is no excuse for the present publicity except for the gratification of idle curiosity and the filling of newspaper space. . . . It is rather an interesting commentary to note the almost universal condemnation of this publicity in the editorial columns. . . . While as a matter of news the lists occupy many pages in the same issue.

According to a Pennsylvania tax collector, "This publicity has done no good whatever, but, on the other hand, has become a source of information used extensively by solicitors for questionable transactions, collection agencies, mail order concerns, bogus charities and competitors in business." A compromise was soon reached: only the names and addresses of those filing returns were made public.

Each year thereafter, the battle for increased or decreased disclosure was fought again. Each new revenue act found a different side victorious. In 1934, Congressman Wright Patman introduced the most controversial and possibly the shortest-lived tax law proposal ever enacted, the so-called "Pink Slip." At the time, Patman stated: "The Government's system of requiring secrecy of income tax returns places the Government in almost the same position as the blind man passing around the hat. The blind man does not know who contributes nor how much." Patman's suggestion, which Congress adopted, required every person who filed an income tax return to "fill out a publicity sheet which could be detached and sent to a separate department and which would be subject to inspection of any citizen at any time. . . . The sheet would contain limited but essential information."

These publicity sheets would show the taxpayer's name and address, income before taxes, total deductions, net income, total tax credits, and tax payable.

These "pink slips" would be available for public inspection for at least three years after filing. Any taxpayer who didn't complete the form would pay a penalty of $5 and the Commissioner would then complete it for him.

The "pink slip" was a short-lived victory for the proponents of income tax disclosure. In response to a furor of public opposition, Congress repealed the new law before anyone could file a single "pink slip." Much of the opposition stemmed from a fear that the information in the forms would help crooks and kidnappers choose the "best" victims. (The Lindbergh kidnapping had occurred shortly after passage of the "pink slip" act.)

From 1934 to 1976, the law regulating disclosure of tax return information remained relatively unchanged. The Secretary of the Treasury could disclose whether a given taxpayer had filed a return. This is a far cry from publishing the entire return, which had originally been the rule. In addition, under the Internal Revenue Code of 1954, individual returns could be inspected "only on the order of the President."

Yet the debate still raged in early 1978. In the hundred-odd years since we established an income tax, the pendulum has swung both ways—from complete disclosure to complete secrecy, and from a single paragraph detailing publicity regulations to the present set of laws with 17 subsections. Current law amounts to a somewhat middle-of-the-road policy on publicity. The Nixon administration's outrages coupled with the American public reaction against big government's eternal shadow over everyone's life have correctly prompted most of today's pressure for increased confidentiality and respect for individual privacy. Today we are fighting "the onrush of 1984."

Yet I sometimes join economic writer Richard Janssen in suffering a twinge of regret when I think of "that simpler time when the country didn't need armies of revenue agents and platoons of computer sleuths to collect taxes. All it needed was a healthy faith in the inherent nosiness of neighbors."

# 5/TAXATION BY CONFESSION

The Sixteenth Amendment "will of necessity have inquisitorial features; it will provide penalties. It will create a complicated machinery.... Business will be hauled into distant courts. Many fines ... will constantly menace the taxpayer. An army of Federal inspectors, spies, and detectives will descend upon the state. They will compel men of business to show their books and disclose their secrets.... They will require statements and affidavits.... The inspector can blackmail the taxpayer ..."

Statement of Richard E. Byrd
March 5, 1910, to the Virginia House of Delegates

The history of the Internal Revenue Service and the history of our tax system parallel the history of the United States involvement in wars. Taxation was a major cause of the American Revolution; the War of 1812 brought the first stirrings of a federal income tax. The agency that became the Internal Revenue Service was created to help finance the Civil War and the income tax was resurrected in anticipation of the American entry into World War I. The Second World War made the income tax a mass phenomenon. The revenue requirements of the cold war, and the federal war on poverty of the 1960s, as well as the national economic depression of the 1970s, only increased the importance of this broad-based revenue producer.

During the American Revolution, itself partly a response to unfair British taxation, the Continental Congress could levy no taxes at all. Instead, the revolution was financed in the most part through debt and theft. Many of today's taxpayers feel that little has changed in the last two hundred years.

When George Washington was still a general he had been forced to steal. While his soldiers went hungry in Valley Forge, nearby farmers took hard cash for their products from the British in Philadelphia. A spirit of profiteering and a habit of graft allowed New York's grain surplus to be diverted to the British in New York City and civilians in New England. Congress capitulated and finally authorized Washington to commandeer needed supplies. On the seas, captains of American ships grew wealthy taking their profits as privateers. Backed with Congressional letters of marque, American shipowners grew rich through privateering rather than commerce.

What could not be stolen was financed through paper currency purchases and debt. Not only Congress, but each colony printed and issued its own paper. The result was massive inflation and, eventually, financial tragedy. On March 15, 1780, Congress declared 40 Continental dollars equal to one in gold—in one step they wiped out $200 million in debt and bankrupted the small wage earner and soldier who were paid in Continental paper.

After independence, under the Articles of Confederation, the central government was again denied the power to tax. It could only borrow and requisition from the individual states. These fiscal requests were frequently ignored and the central government of the Confederation was soon bankrupt. The Constitution of 1789 remedied this by granting the national Congress the power to "levy" and "collect" taxes, duties, imports, and excises.

Congress exercised this new authority in March 1791. Prodded by George Washington and his treasury secretary,

Alexander Hamilton, Congress established a tariff system under which the Treasury Department could collect duties on selected imports and an excise tax on whisky distilling and tobacco products. The government's revenue need was small. National defense required little in the beginning. The government had come into existence with no navy or marine corps to support, and an army reduced to 672 officers and men.

Early Americans, however, did not like centrally imposed taxation, so even George Washington was not spared the challenge of a tax revolt. On August 4, 1794, Supreme Court Justice James Wilson told the first President in a letter that "combinations too powerful to be suppressed by the ordinary course of judicial proceedings had "opposed" and "obstructed" the enforcement of a mild 1791 excise tax on whisky. When a United States marshal had tried to collect the tax in July 1794, his home was burned to the ground and he was beaten by a band of 36 men. Two revenue agents had been tarred and feathered. Those farmers who paid the tax soon saw their stills destroyed by the leaders of this insurrection in the name of the "virtuous principles of republican liberty." The memory of the hated excise taxes imposed by the British Parliament lingered on. The Whisky Tax Rebellion had begun.

In September, Washington acted. Calling up the Pennsylvania, New Jersey, Virginia, and Maryland militias, the president-general and his staff, including Treasury Secretary Alexander Hamilton and Secretary of War Henry Knox, left Philadelphia on September 30 for western Pennsylvania. At the head of 12,900 men, Washington marched into Bedford, the heart of the rebel territory. But no fighting was necessary. The rebels simply dispersed and the uprising was quashed without a skirmish. Although an accidental discharge of a pistol at one point resulted in one death, the occupation of the western counties and the arrest of the leaders of the rebellion were peaceful. Of the twenty leaders arrested and sent to Philadelphia for trial, only two were convicted. They both were later pardoned by President Washington. Thus ended, for the time being, resistance to internal revenue tax measures.

Congress soon added more internal revenue duties. During the Washington and Adams administrations, excise taxes were established on carriages, salt, investments, and sugar refining. Since this scheme of taxation required a collection system, the Office of Commissioner of Revenue was created in 1792. Six years later, Congress provided for the first direct tax. A total levy of $2 million was to be apportioned among the states, as required by the Constitution. The tax covered owners of slaves ($228,000), houses ($457,-000) and land ($1,315,000) but never operated according to original estimates. The rate structure was to be progressive on houses and the tax on each slave was fifty cents. After deducting the resulting payments from the sum apportioned to each state, the remainder was assessed upon the land according to a valuation of each piece at a rate that would produce the given sum. Payments were so much in arrears that after three years, one-fifth of the tax remained unpaid. Total receipts amounted to $734,000 in 1800 and $534,000 in 1801.

Still there was no federal income tax. During the War of 1812, Treasury Secretary Alexander Dallas had suggested one to help finance President Madison's defense against the British. Though he carefully used the word "temporary" in talking about the tax, Congress told him rather rudely to keep his mad thoughts to himself. The war ended, and the subject was not brought up again.

So, for its first century of existence, until 1861, the U.S. federal government depended on three sources for the bulk of its revenues: customs duties, internal excise taxes, and sale of public domain lands in the Midwest and the West. Of these three, customs duties was the most important, providing over $9 million in 1800, while internal revenue yielded $1.5 million and all other sources, $200,000. Even as late as 1850, customs duties totaled $26.5 million; in the same year, internal revenue fell to less than $50,000.

This early system worked well. Incredibly, it even produced a surplus in some years. During the administration of Andrew Jackson, after the federal debt had been liquidated, part of the remaining surplus was returned to the states. The federal government never again allowed itself this luxury.

Then came the Civil War, the first "modern war" and an American fiscal revolution. With the war came reduced customs duties when the southern coastline was blockaded, and a mounting federal debt. The first Civil War revenue measure, passed on August 5, 1861, soon proved inadequate. In the spring of 1862, with public debt climbing at the dizzying rate of $2 million a day, a hesitant Congress was finally prodded into action. It enacted a progessive income tax that was to be the foundation of our present internal revenue system and provided for a Commissioner of Internal Revenue to serve under the Treasury Secretary. President Lincoln signed the bill into law on July 1, 1862.

In addition to taxing incomes, with a provision for tax withholding, the new law taxed estates, public utilities, occupations, banks, insurance companies, railroads and ferries, cattle slaughter, advertisements, and a list of commodities that included liquor, beer, and tobacco. The law also provided for stamp taxes on certain commercial papers, on cosmetics and perfumes, on playing cards, and on medicines.

Two days later, when this historic news was published in the Washington *Evening Star*, equal space was given to a law making polygamy a crime.

The new tax law divided the nation into 185 collection districts, each with an assessor, a collector, deputies, and assistants. The key field officer was the assessor. For a salary of $3 to $5 a day, he kept his office open to hear appeals, issue summonses to delinquent taxpayers, and inspect accounts. The collector, a political appointee, received a commission of up to 50 percent of the amount he collected. These collectors had a reputation of being "enthusiastically pro-government."

President Lincoln appointed George Sewell Boutwell, a Republican lawyer from Massachusetts, as the first Commisioner of Internal Revenue. Although Boutwell brought to the job broad experience as a teacher, legislator, and Governor, he had only an inkling of what was in the new law. As he later reported, "My first labor was to read the ... law, which I had not before seen."

Beginning with three borrowed clerks in a single office in the treasury building, Boutwell had to create a record-keeping system, contract for the printing of revenue stamps, interpret the new law, and issue rulings. He designed the first income tax return shown as Figure 1. It was due the first Monday of each May and had to be "sworn to" in the presence of an assistant assessor. There was no provision for joint filing and the basic tax rate was only 1½ percent.

Boutwell's correspondence was, for the times, voluminous. Because many Americans were worried about how the law would effect them, the new commissioner of Internal Revenue received perhaps 800 letters per day. But Boutwell's true impact on his office and his nation came from his arbitrary arrogation of powers. Before he had been in office five months, he had made more than 100 decisions relating to the principles of the new law, and over 200 rulings. His term lasted less than a year, from July 1862 to March 1863.

Those not satisfied with his actions could have recourse to the courts. Boutwell did his best to avoid court action by operating on the principle that taxes should be levied only in cases "clearly provided for by statute." He consequently ordered agency employees to rule against the government and in favor of the individual whenever there was "a reasonable doubt" as as to how the law should be applied.

By January 1863, Boutwell had 6,882 employees at his disposal. That year he resigned and was replaced by another lawyer, Joseph J. Lewis, a friend of President Lincoln. During Lewis' term, communication within the growing Internal Revenue bureaucracy became a problem. Lewis sometimes ruled one way while the chief of a division was ruling another way on the same issue. Conflicting interpretations between Washington and the field became common.

By 1864 an intense drive to repeal the income tax had begun. Abraham Lincoln himself apologized for the "inequities in the practical application of taxes."

In response to the growing national debt, Congress established a three-person Revenue Commission in 1865 to make recommendations for the future. Treasury Secretary Hugh McCulloch chose David A. Wells to head the study and Samuel S. Hayes and Stephen Colwell to assist him. The commission recommended reductions in the rates of some taxes, the elimination of others, and the retention of the income tax. The commission also found that not all was as it should be with the new agency. Pay scales were lower than those in private industry; appointments were made on the basis of political patronage; and efforts had been made to secure the discharge of service personnel who, in carrying out their duties, had interfered with the private interests of influential persons.

Even that early, many people found the tax code to be too complex. President Lincoln apparently misunderstood the massive law and overpaid by $1,250 the tax on his salary. The tax was refunded to his estate, but not until 1872.

One of the few who seemed to have derived any pleasure out of the Civil War income tax was Mark Twain. In 1864 he paid a tax of $36.82, plus a $3.12 fine for late filing. He remarked happily that the tax made him feel "important";

By the sixth section of the Act of July 1, 1862, it is made the duty of any person liable to the income tax, on or before the first Monday of May in each year, to make a list or return of the amount of his annual income to the assistant assessor of the district in which he or she resides.

Every person who shall fail to make such return by the day specified, will be liable to be assessed by the assessor according to the best information which he can obtain; and in such case the assessor will add fifty per centum to the amount of the items of such list.

Every person who shall deliver to an assessor any false or fraudulent list or statement, with intent to evade the valuation of his income, is subject to a fine of five hundred dollars; and in such case the list will be made out by the assessor or assistant assessor, and from the valuation so made there can be no appeal.

As it is not impossible that certain changes in the rates of income tax may be adopted by the present Congress, the rate to which any income is liable cannot now be stated. The proposed changes, however, will not affect the principles upon which the return is to be made.

In no case, whatever may be the rate of tax to which an income is liable, is a higher rate than 1½ per cent. to be assessed upon that portion of income derived from interest upon notes, bonds, or other securities of the United States. In order to give full effect to this provision, it is directed that when income is derived partly from these and partly from other sources, the $600 and other allowances made by law shall be deducted, as far as possible, from that portion of income derived from other sources.

When a married woman is entitled to an income which is secured to her own use, free from any control of her husband, the return should be made in her own name, and the assessment will be made separate from that made against the husband. Where a husband and wife live together, and their taxable incomes are in excess of $600, they will be entitled to but one deduction of $600 —that being the average fixed by law as an estimated commutation for the expense of maintaining a family. Where they live apart, by divorce or under contract of separation, they will be each entitled to a deduction of $600.

Guardians and trustees, whether such trustees are so by virtue of their office as executors, administrators, or other fiduciary capacity, are required to make return of the income belonging to minors or other persons which may be held by them in trust; and the income tax will be assessed upon the amount returned, after deducting such sums as are exempted by law: Provided, That the exemption of six hundred dollars shall not be allowed on account of any minor or other beneficiary of a trust, except upon the statement of the guardian or trustee, made under oath, that the minor or beneficiary has no other income from which the said amount of six hundred dollars may be exempted and deducted. Every fatherless child who is possessed of an income in his own right is entitled to the exemption.

On the following pages will be found detailed statements to assist in making out returns.

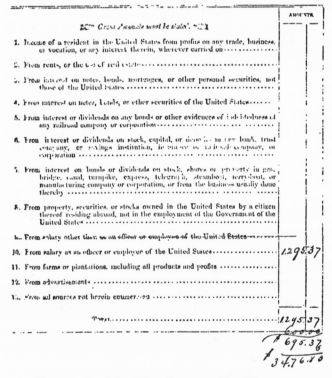

DETAILED STATEMENT OF SOURCES OF INCOME AND THE AMOUNT DERIVED FROM EACH, DURING THE YEAR 1863.

Gross Amounts must be stated.

| | AMOUNTS |
|---|---|
| 1. Income of a resident in the United States from profits on any trade, business, or vocation, or any interest therein, wherever carried on | |
| 2. From rents, or the use of real estate | |
| 3. From interest on notes, bonds, mortgages, or other personal securities, not those of the United States | |
| 4. From interest on notes, bonds, or other securities of the United States | |
| 5. From interest or dividends on any bonds or other evidences of indebtedness of any railroad company or corporation | |
| 6. From interest or dividends on stock, capital, or deposit in any bank, trust company, or savings institution, insurance or railroad company, or corporation | |
| 7. From interest on bonds or dividends on stock, shares or property in gas, bridge, canal, turnpike, express, telegraph, steamboat, ferry-boat, or manufacturing company or corporation, or from the business usually done thereby | |
| 8. From property, securities, or stocks owned in the United States by a citizen thereof residing abroad, not in the employment of the Government of the United States | |
| 9. From salary other than as an officer or employee of the United States | |
| 10. From salary as an officer or employee of the United States | 1,295.37 |
| 11. From farms or plantations, including all products and profits | |
| 12. From advertisements | |
| 13. From all sources not herein enumerated | |
| Total | 1,295.37 |
| | 600.00 |
| | 695.37 |
| | 34.76.80 |

Figure 1   The First Income Tax Form

## DETAILED STATEMENT OF DEDUCTIONS AUTHORIZED TO BE MADE.

| | AMOUNTS |
|---|---|
| 1. Expenses necessarily incurred and paid in carrying on any trade, business or vocation, such as rent of store, clerk hire, insurance, fuel, freight, &c. | |
| 2. Amount actually paid by a property owner for necessary repairs, insurance, and interest on incumbrances upon his property | |
| 3. Amount paid by a farmer or planter for— | |
| (a) Hired labor, including the subsistence of the laborers | |
| (b) Necessary repairs upon his farm or plantation | |
| (c) Insurance, and interest on incumbrances upon his farm or plantation | |
| 4. Other national, state, and local taxes assessed and paid for the year 1863, and not elsewhere included | |
| 5. Amount actually paid for rent of the dwelling-house or estate occupied as a residence | |
| 6. Exempted by law. (except in the case of a citizen of the United States residing abroad,) $600 | 600 00 |
| 7. Income from interest or dividends on stock, capital, or deposits in any bank, trust company, or savings institution, insurance, or railroad company, from which 3 per cent. thereon was withheld by the officers thereof | |
| 8. Income from interest on bonds, or other evidences of indebtedness of any railroad company or corporation, from which 3 per cent. thereon was withheld by the officers thereof | |
| 9. Salaries of officers, or payments to persons in the civil, military, naval, or other service of the United States, in excess of $600 | |
| 10. Income from advertisements, on which 3 per cent. was paid | |
| TOTAL | 600 00 |

I hereby certify that the following is a true and faithful statement of the gains, profits, or income of _____ of the _____ of _____ in the County of _____, and State of _____, whether derived from any kind of property, rents, interest, dividends, salary, or from any profession, trade, employment, or vocation, or from any other source whatever, from the 1st day of January to the 31st day of December, 1863, both days inclusive, and subject to an Income Tax under the excise laws of the United States:

| | RATE. | AMOUNT. | AMOUNT OF TAX |
|---|---|---|---|
| Income subject to | 3 per cent. | 695 37 | 34 76 |
| Do. subject to | 5 per cent. | | |
| Income derived from interest upon notes, bonds, or other securities of the United States, subject to | 1½ per cent. | | |
| Income from property in the United States owned by a citizen thereof residing abroad, subject to | per cent. | | |
| Income exceeding upon a portion of which a tax of 3 per cent. has already been paid, subject to | per cent. | | |
| TOTAL | | | |

(Signed)

John A. Provost.

Dated at _____ this _____ day of _____, 1864.

Sworn and subscribed before me, this 30 day of September, 1864.

Wm M Bennett

Assistant Assessor.

the cold and distant government was at last paying attention to him. Many citizens of a less expansive nature, however, felt they could get along without this cozy feeling that somebody in Washington cared. Nonpayment of the tax filled them with an equally pleasant warmth.

In historical perspective, the overall record of the Office of the Collector of Internal Revenue during the Civil War was an impressive one. Although loans covered 80 percent of the cost of the war, the four-year-old internal revenue agency collected some $311 million in excise, income, and inheritance taxes for fiscal 1866. Income taxes alone provided $79 million. This mark, not to be reached again for forty-five years, should be compared with total federal revenue just fifteen years before—$28.5 million.

In 1865, when the Civil War ended, national debt reached a record $3 billion. But in late 1866 and the following year, Congress reduced or eliminated many taxes. In 1868 the taxation of distilled beverages and tobacco became the major source of internal revenue. This remained the case for the next 45 years.

Congress made occasional taxation experiments, mainly in the use of taxes for "regulatory" purposes. An oleomargarine tax in 1866 was intended less as a revenue source than as a butterfat protection measure.

In 1872, Congress repealed the income tax, even though the Revenue Commission established a few years before had spoken out in favor of it. Congress acted primarily because the income tax had never worked correctly. It was inefficient. The tax law had been amended six times, each change adding to the confusion and self-contradiction. In 1872, less than 73,000 citizens were required to file a return for a tax the *New York Tribune* had called, on February 5, 1869, "the most odious, vexatious, inquisitorial and unequal of all our taxes."

The income tax, however, was not eliminated without a struggle by its supporters, mostly in the states west of the

Alleghenies where fewer people had to pay the tax. As the Southern states reentered the Union in the decades following the war, they joined with the Western states in continued agitation for the reestablishment of an income tax, a tax that would fall mostly on the high-income earners in the Eastern states of New York, Massachusetts, Pennsylvania, and New Jersey. No less than 14 income tax bills were introduced in Congress during the 1870s. During the 1880s, customs receipts and excise taxes on spirits, beer, and tobacco met the federal government's revenue needs so income tax advocates lacked an ideal argument for their cause.

With the beginning of the American expansionist era in 1893, a massive and expensive build-up of the navy became essential. But when President Cleveland followed through on his promise to cut tariffs, the government was left embarrassingly short of revenue. So Cleveland proposed a modest income tax of 2 percent on all incomes in excess of $4,000, provoking horror and outrage among the rich and their representatives in Congress.

"Socialism, communism and devilism!" roared Senator John Sherman, author of the Sherman Antitrust Act. Another senator howled: "If we pass this bill, free enterprise dies on this spot! We shall tax the hardworking and the successful while letting the lazy and improvident go." In the House of Representatives, a congressman called the tax "odious" and "unutterably distasteful both in its moral and material aspects." He predicted: "The imposition of this tax will corrupt the people. It will bring in its train the spy and the informer. It will necessitate a swarm of officials with inquisitorial powers. . . ."

Despite this rhetoric, income tax proponents eventually mustered enough strength to add an income tax amendment to the Wilson Tariff Act of 1894. The measure provided for a 2 percent levy on all net income over $4,000.

The Internal Revenue Bureau soon established an Income

Tax Division to administer the tax. But one year later, in 1895, before the tax returns had even been printed, the constitutionality of the new law was challenged in the case of *Pollock* v. *Farmers Loan & Trust Company.* The Supreme Court had to decide whether the new income tax was a "direct tax," in which case the Constitution mandated that it be apportioned among the states on the basis of population. Of course, income tax apportionment was a political impossibility, since in a populous state where incomes were low, apportionment could have required a low-income taxpayer to pay a higher tax than a wealthy taxpayer in a less populous state.

Even though the Court, just 15 years before, had approved the Civil War income tax, finding it similar to an excise tax or duty, and even though there were some indications that the Founding Fathers had considered only poll taxes and taxes on land to be direct taxes requiring apportionment, the Supreme Court struck down the income tax as unconstitutionally direct. Apparently accepting charges that the income tax was communistic and socialistic, the Court reasoned that a tax on the income from property was equivalent to a direct tax on property itself, and therefore had to be apportioned.

"This is class legislation," grumbled Justice Stephen J. Field, branding the law discriminatory and unfair because it would tax the rich more than the poor. Such legislation, he said, "leads inevitably to oppression and abuses and to general unrest and disturbances in society." He grumpily likened the tax to an early British one in which Protestants paid one rate, Catholics twice that much, Jews still more.

Justice Field saw the tax as the beginning of an assault upon capital and a steppingstone to other attacks "till our political contests will become a war of the poor against the rich." Justice Henry B. Brown, who had voted for the income tax, saw its defeat as "nothing less than a surrender of the taxing power to the moneyed class." A few months later, the Income Tax Division of the Internal Revenue Bureau was disbanded.

The income tax issue was kept alive by political activists of both major political parties, by the leaders of such splinter groups as the Greenback, Populist, and Anti-Monopoly parties and by a number of popular writers. In 1909, a coalition against the income tax, consisting mostly of wealthy Eastern Republicans, and the income tax proponents in Congress hammered out a compromise. Working through Republican President William Howard Taft, who presented the plan to Congress in a presidential message, the opponents favored a 1 percent excise tax on corporations with a net income of over $5,000 and the initiation of an amendment to the Constitution that would empower Congress to tax incomes "without apportionment among the several States." The opponents of the income tax hoped the Supreme Court would invalidate this proposed excise tax as a disguised direct income tax and that the requisite three-fourths of the states would not ratify the proposed amendment. It looked like a shrewd political maneuver: It would defuse agitation for an individual and perhaps a corporate income tax and the mild tax it did establish would not survive.

The plan blew up. In 1911, the Supreme Court, in *Flint* v. *Stone Tracy Company,* held the new levy to be a constitutional excise tax which did *not* require apportionment, unlike the income tax of 1894.

Moreover, two years later Wyoming became the 36th state to ratify the Sixteenth Amendment, making it part of the Constitution and eliminating the whole apportionment problem. In October 1913, Congress enacted the Revenue Act of 1913, retroactive to March 1, 1913. Since then the progressive income tax has been part of the American federal tax structure.

A correspondence unit with 30 employees was quickly established to handle the flood of questions about the new law, and the Bureau of Internal Revenue began drafting regulations, preparing necessary forms, and training its staff in the new procedures. (Figure 2)

The new income tax law provided for withholding most of the taxes that would now be due. This withholding scheme was repealed in 1916 and did not emerge again until 1943.

The new tax was a harbinger of complexities to come. It essentially provided for a normal tax of 1 percent on incomes of $3,000 to $20,000 (the starting point was $4,000 for a married taxpayer), with a modest surtax on incomes above that level. The highest surtax was six percent, on incomes over $500,000. There was also a 1 percent tax on corporate income.

The *New York Times* editorialized on April 12, 1913, that the new tax had "transferred the burdens of the many to the shoulders of the few." The *Times* grumbled that the new law "will tax the honest and let the dishonest escape." It found the law so complicated that it discriminated unjustly against those who were poor at mathematics. Moreover, rejecting promises that the tax was temporary, the *Times* pessimistically predicted that the rates would eventually double, to an outrageous two percent!

One immediate effect of the Sixteenth Amendment was the enlargement of the Internal Revenue Bureau. The Personal Income Tax Division was reestablished containing the correspondence unit of 30 employees, who answered the public's questions concerning the law and its enforcement. In order to explain the personal income tax, the agency began a broad public education program. By the end of 1913, the Bureau employed 277 persons in Washington, D.C., and 3,723 in the field; two years later, the Washington staff had ballooned to 531, the field force to 4,280.

In 1914, the Internal Revenue Bureau collected $380 million in *total* taxes, including the new income tax. The average individual federal tax payment that year was a massive $3.88.

From 1872 to 1913, the Bureau of Internal Revenue had

| TO BE FILLED IN BY COLLECTOR. | Form 1040. | TO BE FILLED IN BY INTERNAL REVENUE BUREAU. |
|---|---|---|

**INCOME TAX.**

List No. ........................

............ District of ............................

Date received ..........................................

**THE PENALTY**
FOR FAILURE TO HAVE THIS RETURN IN
THE HANDS OF THE COLLECTOR OF
INTERNAL REVENUE ON OR BEFORE
MARCH 1 IS $20 TO $1,000.
(SEE INSTRUCTIONS ON PAGE 4.)

File No. ...................................................

Assessment List ...................................

Page ...................... Line ....................

### UNITED STATES INTERNAL REVENUE.

### RETURN OF ANNUAL NET INCOME OF INDIVIDUALS.
(As provided by Act of Congress, approved October 3, 1913.)

**RETURN OF NET INCOME RECEIVED OR ACCRUED DURING THE YEAR ENDED DECEMBER 31, 191....**
(FOR THE YEAR 1913, FROM MARCH 1, TO DECEMBER 31.)

Filed by (or for) ......................................................................... of ............................................................
(Full name of individual.) (Street and No.)

In the City, Town, or Post Office of .......................................................... State of ...........................
(Fill in pages 2 and 3 before making entries below.)

1. GROSS INCOME (see page 2, line 12) ............................................................... $............

2. GENERAL DEDUCTIONS (see page 3, line 7) ........................................................ $............

3. NET INCOME .............................................................................................. $............

Deductions and exemptions allowed in computing income subject to the normal tax of 1 per cent.

4. Dividends and net earnings received or accrued, of corporations, etc., subject to like tax. (See page 2, line 11)......... $............

5. Amount of income on which the normal tax has been deducted and withheld at the source. (See page 2, line 9, column A)..

6. Specific exemption of $3,000 or $4,000, as the case may be. (See Instructions 3 and 19) ......................................

Total deductions and exemptions. (Items 4, 5, and 6)......... $............

7. TAXABLE INCOME on which the normal tax of 1 per cent is to be calculated. (See Instruction 3).. $............

8. When the net income shown above on line 3 exceeds $20,000, the additional tax thereon must be calculated as per schedule below:

| | | | | INCOME. | | | | TAX. | | | |
|---|---|---|---|---|---|---|---|---|---|---|---|
| 1 per cent on amount over $20,000 and not exceeding $50,000.... | | | | $............ | | | | $............ | | | |
| 2 " " 50,000 " " 75,000.... | | | | | | | | | | | |
| 3 " " 75,000 " " 100,000.... | | | | | | | | | | | |
| 4 " " 100,000 " " 250,000.... | | | | | | | | | | | |
| 5 " " 250,000 " " 500,000.... | | | | | | | | | | | |
| 6 " " 500,000 .... | | | | | | | | | | | |

Total additional or super tax ....................................... $............

Total normal tax (1 per cent of amount entered on line 7).... $............

Total tax liability............................................... $............

## Figure 2 The 1913 Income Tax Form

**2**

## GROSS INCOME.

*This statement must show in the proper spaces the entire amount of gains, profits, and income received by or accrued to the individual from all sources during the year specified on page 1.*

| DESCRIPTION OF INCOME. | A. Amount of income on which tax has been deducted and withheld at the source. | | | | | B. Amount of income on which tax has not been deducted and withheld at the source. | | | | |
|---|---|---|---|---|---|---|---|---|---|---|
| 1. Total amount derived from salaries, wages, or compensation for personal service of whatever kind and in whatever form paid. | $ | | | | | $ | | | | |
| 2. Total amount derived from professions, vocations, businesses, trade, commerce, or sales or dealings in property, whether real or personal, growing out of the ownership or use of or interest in real or personal property, including bonds, stocks, etc. | | | | | | | | | | |
| 3. Total amount derived from rents and from interest on notes, mortgages, and securities (other than reported on lines 5 and 6). | | | | | | | | | | |
| 4. Total amount of gains and profits derived from partnership business, whether the same be divided and distributed or not. | | | | | | | | | | |
| 5. Total amount of fixed and determinable annual gains, profits, and income derived from interest upon bonds and mortgages or deeds of trust, or other similar obligations of corporations, joint-stock companies or associations, and insurance companies, whether payable annually or at shorter or longer periods. | | | | | | | | | | |
| 6. Total amount of income derived from coupons, checks, or bills of exchange for or in payment of interest upon bonds issued in *foreign countries* and upon *foreign mortgages* or like obligations (not payable in the United States), and also from coupons, checks, or bills of exchange for or in payment of any dividends upon the stock or interest upon the obligations of foreign corporations, associations, and insurance companies engaged in business in foreign countries. | | | | | | | | | | |
| 7. Total amount of income received from fiduciaries. | | | | | | | | | | |
| 8. Total amount of income derived from any source whatever, not specified or entered elsewhere on this page. | | | | | | | | | | |
| 9. TOTALS. | $ | | | | | $ | | | | |
| NOTE.—Enter total of Column A on line 5 of first page. | | | | | | | | | | |
| 10. AGGREGATE TOTALS OF COLUMNS A AND B | | | | | | $ | | | | |
| 11. Total amount of income derived from dividends on the stock or from the net earnings of corporations, joint-stock companies, associations, or insurance companies subject to like tax (To be entered on line 4 of first page.) | | | | | | $ | | | | |
| 12. TOTAL "Gross Income" (to be entered on line 1 of first page). | | | | | | $ | | | | |

**3**

## GENERAL DEDUCTIONS.

| | | | | | |
|---|---|---|---|---|---|
| 1. The amount of necessary expenses actually paid in carrying on business, but not including business expenses of partnerships, and not including personal, living, or family expenses...... | $......... | .......... | .......... | ...... | |
| 2. All interest paid within the year on personal indebtedness of taxpayer........................ | .......... | .... ..... | .......... | ...... | |
| 3. All national, State, county, school, and municipal taxes paid within the year (not including those assessed against local benefits),.......................................................... | .......... | .......... | .......... | ...... | |
| 4. Losses actually sustained during the year incurred in trade or arising from fires, storms, or shipwreck, and not compensated for by insurance or otherwise ......... ................. ....| .......... | .......... | .......... | ...... | |
| 5. Debts due which have been actually ascertained to be worthless and which have been charged off within the year............................................................................ | .......... | .......... | .......... | ...... | |
| 6. Amount representing a reasonable allowance for the exhaustion, wear, and tear of property arising out of its use or employment in the business, not to exceed, in the case of mines, 5 per cent of the gross value at the mine of the output for the year for which the computation is made, but no deduction shall be made for any amount of expense of restoring property or making good the exhaustion thereof, for which an allowance is or has been made......... | .......... | .......... | .......... | ...... | |
| 7. Total "GENERAL DEDUCTIONS" (to be entered on line 2 of first page) ......................... | .......... | .......... | .......... | ...... | |

### AFFIDAVIT TO BE EXECUTED BY INDIVIDUAL MAKING HIS OWN RETURN.

I solemnly swear (or affirm) that the foregoing return, to the best of my knowledge and belief, contains a true and complete statement of all gains, profits, and income received by or accrued to me during the year for which the return is made, and that I am entitled to all the deductions and exemptions entered or claimed therein, under the Federal Income-tax Law of October 3, 1913.

Sworn to and subscribed before me this..........................

day of ..............................., 191

‾‾‾‾‾‾‾‾‾‾‾‾‾‾‾‾‾‾‾‾‾‾‾‾‾‾‾‾‾‾‾‾‾‾‾‾
(Signature of individual.)

SEAL OF
OFFICER
TAKING
AFFIDAVIT.

‾‾‾‾‾‾‾‾‾‾‾‾‾‾‾‾‾‾‾‾‾‾‾‾‾‾‾‾‾‾‾‾‾‾‾‾
(Official capacity.)

### AFFIDAVIT TO BE EXECUTED BY DULY AUTHORIZED AGENT MAKING RETURN FOR INDIVIDUAL.

I solemnly swear (or affirm) that I have sufficient knowledge of the affairs and property of ................................................
to enable me to make a full and complete return thereof, and that the foregoing return, to the best of my knowledge and belief, contains a true and complete statement of all gains, profits, and income received by or accrued to said individual during the year for which the return is made, and that the said individual is entitled, under the Federal Income-tax Law of October 3, 1913, to all the deductions and exemptions entered or claimed therein.

Sworn to and subscribed before me this..........................

day of ..............................., 191

‾‾‾‾‾‾‾‾‾‾‾‾‾‾‾‾‾‾‾‾‾‾‾‾‾‾‾‾‾‾‾‾‾‾‾‾
(Signature of agent.)

ADDRESS
IN FULL.

SEAL OF
OFFICER
TAKING
AFFIDAVIT.

‾‾‾‾‾‾‾‾‾‾‾‾‾‾‾‾‾‾‾‾‾‾‾‾‾‾‾‾‾‾‾‾‾‾‾‾
(Official capacity.)

c 2—7357

[SEE INSTRUCTIONS ON BACK OF THIS PAGE.]

**4**

## INSTRUCTIONS.

1. This return shall be made by every citizen of the United States, whether residing at home or abroad, and by every person residing in the United States, though not a citizen thereof, having a *net income* of $3,000 or over for the taxable year, and *also* by every *nonresident alien* deriving income from property owned and business, trade, or profession carried on *in the United States* by him.

2. When an individual by reason of minority, sickness or other disability, or absence from the United States, is unable to make his own return, it may be made for him by his *duly authorized* representative.

3. The *normal tax* of 1 per cent shall be assessed on the total net income less the specific exemption of $3,000 or $4,000 as the case may be. (For the year 1913, the specific exemption allowable is $2,500 or $3,333.33, as the case may be.) If, however, the normal tax has been deducted and withheld on any part of the income at the source, or if any part of the income is received as dividends upon the stock or from the net earnings of any corporation, etc., which is taxable upon its net income, such income shall be deducted from the individual's total *net income* for the purpose of calculating the amount of income on which the individual is liable for the normal tax of 1 per cent by virtue of this return. (See page 1, line 7.)

4. The *additional or super tax* shall be calculated as stated on page 1.

5. This return shall be filed with the Collector of Internal Revenue for the district in which the individual resides if he has no other place of business, otherwise in the district in which he has his *principal place of business;* or in case the person resides in a foreign country, then with the collector for the district in which his principal business is carried on in the United States.

6. This return must be filed on or before the first day of March succeeding the close of the calendar year for which return is made.

7. The *penalty for failure to file the return within the time specified by law* is $20 to $1,000. In case of refusal or neglect to render the return within the required time (except in cases of sickness or absence), 50 per cent shall be added to amount of tax assessed. In case of *false or fraudulent return*, 100 per cent shall be added to such tax, and any person required by law to make, render, sign, or verify any return who makes any false or fraudulent return or statement with intent to defeat or evade the assessment required by this section to be made shall be guilty of a misdemeanor, and shall be fined not exceeding $2,000 or be imprisoned not exceeding one year, or both, at the discretion of the court, with the costs of prosecution.

8. When the return is not filed within the required time by reason of sickness or absence of the individual, an extension of time, not exceeding 30 days from March 1, within which to file such return, *may be* granted by the collector, *provided* an application therefor is made by the individual within the period for which such extension is desired.

9. This return properly filled out must be made under oath or affirmation. Affidavits may be made before any officer *authorized by law* to administer oaths. If before a justice of the peace or magistrate, not using a seal, *a certificate of the clerk of the court as to the authority* of such officer to administer oaths should be *attached to the return.*

10. Expense for medical attendance, store accounts, family supplies, wages of domestic servants, cost of board, room, or house rent for family or personal use, *are not expenses that can be deducted from gross income.* In case an individual owns his own residence he can not deduct the estimated value of his rent,

neither shall he be required to include such estimated rental of his home as income.

11. The farmer, in computing the net income from his farm for his annual return, shall include all moneys received for produce and animals sold, and for the wool and hides of animals slaughtered, provided such wool and hides are sold, and he shall deduct therefrom the sums actually paid as purchase money for the animals sold or slaughtered during the year.

When animals were raised by the owner and are sold or slaughtered he shall not deduct their value as expenses or loss. He may deduct the amount of money actually paid as expense for producing any farm products, live stock, etc. In deducting expenses for repairs on farm property the amount deducted must not exceed the amount actually expended for such repairs during the year for which the return is made. (See page 3, item 6.) The cost of replacing tools or machinery is a deductible expense to the extent that the cost of the new articles does not exceed the value of the old.

12. In calculating losses, only such losses as shall have been actually sustained and the amount of which has been definitely ascertained during the year covered by the return can be deducted.

13. Persons receiving fees or emoluments for professional or other services, as in the case of physicians or lawyers, should include all actual receipts for services rendered in the year for which return is made, together with all unpaid accounts, charges for services, or contingent income due for that year, if good and collectible.

14. Debts which were contracted during the year for which return is made, but found in said year to be worthless, may be deducted from gross income for said year, but such debts can not be regarded as worthless until after legal proceedings to recover the same have proved fruitless, or it clearly appears that the debtor is insolvent. If debts contracted prior to the year for which return is made were included as income in return for year in which said debts were contracted, and such debts shall subsequently prove to be worthless, they may be deducted under the head of losses in the return for the year in which such debts were charged off as worthless.

15. Amounts due or accrued to the individual members of a partnership from the net earnings of the partnership, whether apportioned and distributed or not, shall be included in the annual return of the individual.

16. United States pensions shall be included as income.

17. Estimated advance in value of real estate is not required to be reported as income, unless the increased value is taken up on the books of the individual as an increase of assets.

18. Costs of suits and other legal proceedings arising from ordinary business may be treated as an expense of such business, and may be deducted from gross income for the year in which such costs were paid.

19. An unmarried individual or a married individual not living with wife or husband shall be allowed an exemption of $3,000. When husband and wife live together they shall be allowed jointly a total exemption of only $4,000 on their aggregate income. They may make a joint return, both subscribing thereto, or if they have separate incomes, they may make separate returns; but in no case shall they jointly claim more than $4,000 exemption on their aggregate income.

20. In computing net income there shall be excluded the compensation of all officers and employees of a State or any political subdivision thereof, except when such compensation is paid by the United States Government.        o 2–7367

collected customs duties and administered internal revenue duties on liquor and tobacco. Much of its staff, though, had performed essentially nonrevenue functions assigned the agency by Congress. The Bureau of Internal Revenue had protected the butter interests by levying oleomargarine taxes; it had protected American morals by enforcing a tax on opium. During the 1890s the Internal Revenue Bureau's diverse responsibilities also included granting residence certificates to Chinese laborers, and issuing bounties to sugar producers. In 1902 Congress authorized the Internal Revenue Commissioner to sell stamps to show payment of certain excise taxes, such as the one on liquor, as well as to carry out some banking duties for the Treasury Department. In short, the government had used internal taxes primarily to regulate trade in certain items rather than to produce revenue.

The German march into Belgium in 1914 not only changed the face of the world map but triggered a new era in federal taxation as well. To fund pre-World War I war measures, Congress passed the Revenue Act of 1916, raising income tax rates, placing new taxes on estates, stock dividens, and munitions manufacturers' profits, and providing for publication of income tax statistics. Secretary of the Treasury William G. McAdoo warned Congress that the 1916 act would be inadequate, leaving the government with a deficit of about $185 million by 1918. Congress soon responded with the Revenue Act of 1917, raising many tax rates.

When the United States finally entered the war in 1917, the effect on the Internal Revenue Bureau was dramatic. President Wilson demanded higher taxes, and Congress passed the Revenue Act of 1918. This measure codified all existing tax laws, raised rates for the highest tax brackets to a stunning 77 percent, added new excise taxes, established excess profits and estate taxes, and provided for a tax on child labor. This last provision was declared unconstitutional in 1922. In 1920 the Bureau collected $5.5 billion, over 15 times the $344 million it had collected just seven years before.

"The fiscal year of 1918," said Commissioner of Internal Revenue Daniel C. Roper in his annual report, "marks the beginning of a new era of internal revenue taxation." This observation was a gross understatement. At the turn of the century, internal revenue collections of $207 million had just passed collections of $185 million in custom duties. By 1925, when the dust had settled after the repeal and reduction of many World War I levies, internal revenue was producing $3.2 billion and customs a paltry $464 million. From World War I onward, customs duties were never again to constitute anything more than a minor source of federal revenue.

During the war, the bureau added a Capital Stock Division, a Sales Tax Unit, and an Intelligence Division which prevented and uncovered tax fraud. At about the same time, the bureau made several changes to improve the quality and efficiency of service: it established branch offices in major cities, created eleven new collection districts, instituted new accounting and office procedures, extended and reorganized its field service, and started a correspondence study program for bureau employees.

In 1919, after ratification of the Eighteenth Amendment, Congress assigned the Internal Revenue Bureau the task of enforcing Prohibition. To do this, the bureau created two new branches, one to enforce the penal and regulatory provisions of the law, the second to supervise permitted traffic in nonbeverage alcohol. Altogether, the bureau increased its work force by over 4,000 people to enforce prohibition.

In February 1924, Senator James Couzens accused the Internal Revenue Bureau of "improper organization or gross inefficiency" resulting in "lost millions of dollars," "corruption," and conditions under which "taxpayers have been and still are oppressed." As a result of his disclosures, a special congressional committee was formed to investigate the bureau. It revealed a bureaucracy where division heads were supreme and lack of communication left "their superiors in ignorance of how the law is really administered." The committee condemned this "delegation of almost unlimited discretion" which was "secretly exercised," and found that it was "the consistent policy of the Commissioner of Internal Revenue to exceed the authority delegated [to him] to compromise taxes." The committee recommended tax simplification and a streamlining of Internal Revenue procedures. This Joint Committee on Internal Revenue Tax was composed of ten members (five each from the House Ways and Means Committee and the Senate Finance Committee) and still serves Congress by preparing special studies on tax problems and reports on tax systems.

The 1920 election of Republican President Warren G. Harding ushered in a new era in governmental fiscal theory, an era which was to last for a decade and which was personified by Secretary of the Treasury Andrew Mellon. In 1924, when income tax collections were producing an annual surplus of $300 million above budgeted expenses, Mellon argued that a balanced budget was a national necessity and that the maximum income surtax rate should be 25 percent rather than 58 percent, as it then was. He stated that, in general, a high tax rate adversely "affects the prosperity of the country." At Mellon's urging, the government cut taxes five times during the 1920s despite a large outstanding debt, which amounted to $21.6 billion in 1924. By 1932 annual collections amounted to only $1.5 billion, the lowest figure in fifteen years. With decreased taxes and enforcement, the bureau cut its staff by 4,692 people in fiscal 1926. The Mellon era ended with the stock market crash of 1929. With the crash came economic depression and, in 1932, the election of Franklin D. Roosevelt to the presidency. Roosevelt's New Deal marked the beginning of vast deficit spending by the federal government. In 1935, the Social

Security Act was passed and the new Social Security taxes now had to be collected. Increases in estate tax rates and the establishment of a federal gift tax only added to the agency's workload.

The New Deal programs of "relief recovery, and reform" required some administrative reorganization in the Internal Revenue Bureau. The major revision was the creation of a Social Security Tax Division, with a variety of subdivisions. The Bureau of Internal Revenue was also given responsibility in the Work Projects Administration. Altogether, New Deal programs increased the bureau's staff from 11,500 in 1933 to 27,230 in 1941.

In December 1941, the Japanese attacked Pearl Harbor and the United States entered World War II. The demands of that war brought forth a new age of consciousness in taxpaying. The war had to be financed and the principal tax device used to meet these unprecedented revenue demands was to be the income tax. It was to grow from a tax on the "rich" to a broad-based financial drain on almost every wage earner.

The Revenue Act of 1942 sharply increased the income tax rate and raised excise taxes on telephones, telegraph and radio service, liquor, cameras, and perfumes. In the same year, Congress also enacted the Victory Tax, a supplement to the individual income tax, and replaced the excess-profit tax on corporations with a 90 percent tax on all corporate profits. Excise taxes on tobacco and travel were also increased and the estate tax was made more restrictive.

For the 1939 fiscal year, 6.5 million individuals had provided $1 billion of income tax revenue and 550,000 corporations $1.1 billion. Excise taxes produced an additional $1.9 billion, almost as much as the income tax. But because of the progressive income tax, taxpayers with incomes under $5,000 accounted for only 10 percent of total income tax revenue. Even under the new higher rates, a married taxpayer with two dependents and an income of $5,000 paid a federal income tax of approximately $75 (1.5 percent). The war would relegate these sums to ancient history.

The collection process itself was changed with the reintroduction of tax withholding on salaries and wages. Under the withholding system set up in 1943 and still in use today, each employee files a "W-4" form with his employer indicating the number of exemptions claimed. The employer must then withhold a specified percentage of the employee's paychecks, depending on how much tax the employee will owe. The employer must remit the amounts withheld to the Internal Revenue Service. Corporations, individuals with income other than salary and wages, and other taxpayers not subject to withholding must estimate their income for the year and pay their income tax in four installments. Under either arrangement, taxes are paid throughout the year as income is earned.

By the end of the war the narrow base of just over 7 million taxpayers had broadened substantially. In 1945, 48 million individuals paid over $19 billion in income taxes; 603,000 corporations provided $16 billion in revenue; and excise taxes yielded an additional $6.3 billion. The end of the war, though, brought tax cuts in 1945 and 1948.

The wartime tax measures had severely strained the administrative forces of the Internal Revenue Bureau, and, in 1946, Treasury Secretary John W. Snyder called a conference of Internal Revenue Bureau collectors and revenue agents to suggest plans for improvement of bureau operations. Among the suggestions made at this conference and eventually adopted were a revision of internal forms, creation of a microfilm recordkeeping system, reduction of interest payments through careful scheduling of refunds, and the use of preassembled forms when applicable.

One of the first steps toward bureau reorganization was a work simplification program starting at the lowest level of management and working up. The bureau also instituted an Employee Awards system to give workers an incentive to offer suggestions for improvements.

In 1948 the Treasury Department established a special committee to improve the bureau's management. Congress also acted in this matter: the House Committee on Appropriations and the Advisory Group to the Joint Committee on Internal Revenue Taxation submitted a set of recommendations, all of which were gradually implemented.

That year, Treasury Secretary Synder established a committee to direct management studies of the bureau to improve its operating efficiency. According to the report of Secretary Synder, the committee "afforded valuable consultative assistance to the Commissioner in the analysis of possible solutions for management problems." In September 1948, Congress commissioned the management consulting firm of Cresap, McCormick and Paget to study the bureau further. A year later, these consultants presented a report which comprehensively analyzed the Internal Revenue Bureau's organization and procedures.

The culmination of all of these actions was the formal reorganization plan President Truman presented to Congress in 1952. This plan provided for the organization of the bureau on a decentralized basis, rather than on the basis of the type of tax to be administered. Groups were to be organized on the basis of the function of the activity—for example, audit, collection, or internal collection—rather than on the basis of the individual revenue statute to be enforced. In addition, the agency's name was changed from the Bureau of Internal Revenue to the Internal Revenue Service in an effort to emphasize the taxpayer service aspect of the agency's administration of the internal revenue laws.

Another basic change occurred as new lines of responsibility were drawn. Three assistant commissioners were created—one for field operations, another for inspection activities, and the third for technical tax work. In addition, the plan provided for an assistant commissioner to head the management staff, an administrative assistant, an information officer, technical reviewer, and the chief counsel.

This increased complexity in the Internal Revenue Service management was a result of the increased complexity in the law itself. It was overhauled, rewritten, and recodified into the Internal Revenue Code of 1954. Substantive amendments were made in the Revenue Acts of 1958, 1962, 1964, 1966, 1969, 1971, and 1975. The Tax Reform Act of 1976 imposed many major tax changes and, even as this book was being written, the Tax Code was being revised again, this time by the "Tax Simplification Act of 1977," and President Carter's tax package of 1978. Unfortunately, tax simplification has not been the result of the 1977 Act, and probably will escape the 1978 proposals as well. A March 23, 1978 report by Victor Lowe, a division director of the General Accounting Office, revealed that *Internal Revenue advisors* were still providing the wrong answer to one out of every 10 questions asked by taxpayers.

Each time the United States went to war our country's revenue requirements became greater and so did the complexity of the income tax code and the structure of the agency that enforces it.

# 6/GETTING ORGANIZED CRIME

Our Government is a potent, omnipotent teacher for good or for ill. It teaches the whole people by its example. If the Government becomes a law breaker, it breeds contempt for the law; it invites every man to become a law unto himself; it invites anarchy. To declare that in the administration of our laws that the end justifies the means would bring terrible retribution.

Supreme Court Justice Louis Brandeis

To the Chicago police, Al Capone was untouchable. Capone, a gross killer with gargantuan appetites for food, liquor, gambling, and women, would eventually admit to police payoffs in excess of $30,000,000 a year. Over half the metropolitan and county police force was on his payroll. Chicago's mayor, William Hale "Big Bill" Thompson, had been elected with help from a war chest to which Capone had contributed $260,000.

Capone could afford all this. By the end of 1928 he had extorted his way to control of over 91 Chicago unions and trade associations. He ruled bakers and plumbers, movies, and retail food and fruit outlets. He dominated the cleaning and dyeing industry as well as the clerks at city hall. This was in addition to his income from prohibition liquor, gambling, and prostitution. He was earning more than $105,-000,000 a year.

Capone, the killer, the pimp, the extorter, was shielded too well to be convicted of those crimes. But he had failed to pay the tax due on much of his bloated income—and he was ultimately brought down by a branch of the Internal Revenue Service headed by a civil servant whose starting salary a few years before was $150 a month. IRS Commissioner Daniel Roper had established the Special Intelligence Unit in 1919, in response to growing doubts about the inherent honesty of the American taxpayer and the incorruptibility of IRS employees. Roper recruited Elmer Irey, an experienced Post Office inspector from Lynchburg, Virginia, as head of the new department.

At first, the Special Intelligence Unit was responsible only for the investigation and elimination of collusion between taxpayers and tax collectors, but by 1929 the Treasury Department had authorized Irey's agency to investigate any crime related to the federal income tax.

An order from President Hoover himself brought the Special Intelligence Unit into the Capone case. Exactly why the president issued the order to "Get Capone" is still unclear.

According to a story circulated at the time, Hoover had gone to Florida immediately after his election as president of the United States. He and some friends entered a hotel lobby where they were greeted in a manner befitting a president-elect. Suddenly, though, Hoover became a forgotten man. The public's adulation had quickly shifted to another man who was crossing the lobby floor. That man was Scarface Al Capone and, legend has it, this incident led Hoover to send out the order to stop Capone, the man who had upstaged him.

Hoover himself denied the story. Irey later quoted Hoover

as saying: "That story about Florida is absolutely untrue. I never saw Capone in Florida. I always wanted to see something done about Capone and when Frank Knox led a delegation of Chicago citizens to the White House to ask for federal help, I determined that they would get it. That's when I gave the order to put Capone in jail."

Soon after the Special Intelligence Unit's investigation of Al Capone began, Treasury Secretary Andrew Mellon called Irey into his office and asked him if he knew about Hoover's "Brain Trust" which gathered at the White House each morning for exercise and a discussion of the future course of the nation.

Mellon described to Irey how each of these daily sessions started and finished: "Well," he explained, "when the exercising starts Mr. Hoover says 'Have you got that fellow Capone, yet?' And when the exercise is done and everybody is leaving, the last thing Mr. Hoover always says is 'Remember, now; I want that man Capone in jail.'" Whatever motivated Hoover's interest in convicting Capone, the story is an early example of presidential involvement in a specific IRS case.

Another possible reason for Irey's involvement, though, was interdepartmental politics. The Justice Department had its own investigation arm, the Federal Bureau of Investigation. But if Treasury's Internal Revenue Service did the investigation, and Al Capone could be convicted and sent to jail, the Justice Department would take the credit for prosecuting Capone; if the investigation failed, the blame would fall on Treasury. Capone's capture and conviction was ultimately a credit to both departments. The rationale for assigning the case to the Special Intelligence Unit rather than the FBI was Irey's success in gathering evidence on Capone's brother, Ralph, who had signed four delinquent tax returns and then refused to pay the $4,056.75 he admitted owing. Ralph Capone had agreed to the liability and then tried to "cheat, swindle, and defraud" the government when he had over $25,000 in the bank. His cupidity had cost him a $10,000 fine and three years in jail.

Al Capone's syndicate was infiltrated by Pat O'Rourke, an Internal Revenue Service spy. The gangster was to be charged with the crime of tax evasion, on the ground that his net expenditures and net worth would have required income far beyond what he had declared on his tax returns.

Capone was paying $3,000 a year to the telephone company; his suits cost $135 apiece, his shirts $35. The IRS investigators tabulated all of Capone's purchases. He had spent in excess of $72,000 on Western Union orders used for unsuccessful race track bets. Yet Capone could be convinced to admit incomes of only $40,000 in 1927, $26,000 in 1926 and less than $100,000 in 1928 and 1929. Until then he was supposedly struggling along on not more than $75 a week. Capone also confessed to receiving a sixth of his syndicate's profits, which he said accounted for his annual income almost reaching $100,000 in 1928 and 1929.

In May 1931, based on evidence gathered by Internal Revenue Service investigators, a grand jury handed down indictments charging Alphonse Capone with 22 counts of tax evasion. The government could prove only a fraction of Capone's actual income, but that fraction of unreported earnings was as follows:

| Year | Income | Tax |
|------|--------|-----|
| 1924 | $123,101.89 | $32,439.24 |
| 1925 | 257,285.98 | 55,365.25 |
| 1926 | 195,676.00 | 39,962.75 |
| 1927 | 218,056.04 | 45,557.76 |
| 1928 | 140,535.93 | 25,887.72 |
| 1929 | 103,999.00 | 15,817.76 |

Penalties on the above amounts totaled $164,445.09.

Capone's trial began October 6 and lasted ten days. The jury was out ten hours and returned its verdict at 11:10 P.M., October 18. The jury found Capone not guilty of tax evasion for 1924, 1928, and 1929. He was guilty of tax evasion for 1925, 1926, and 1927, and of failing to file returns for 1928 and 1929. Though the conviction for failure to file might seem inconsistent with an acquittal on tax evasion charges for the same two years, the government was satisfied with the outcome.

Had Irey been susceptible to bribery, Al Capone might have received no sentence at all. After dropping an early plan to hire five hoodlums to murder Irey, Capone decided to try bribery instead: the government investigator was promised $1,500,000 in cash if the gangster got off without a jail sentence. Irey rejected the deal and threw Capone's messenger out of his office.

On June 16, 1931, Capone thought he finally had an arrangement. He had agreed with a United States district attorney to plead guilty to all charges in exchange for a compromise two and a half year sentence. But Judge James H. Wilkerson refused to go along and rejected the recommendation of the Justice Department prosecutor. Capone immediately withdrew his plea.

On October 24, Judge Wilkerson sentenced Capone to eleven years in prison, fined him $50,000, and charged him an additional $30,000 for court costs. What the combined efforts of state, county, and municipal law enforcement agencies had been unable to do, put Al Capone in jail and out of business, the Internal Revenue Service Special Intelligence Unit successfully accomplished.

But organized crime was not restricted to Chicago. In New York, Capone's counterpart was Irving Wexler, a bootlegger, strikebreaker, and dope peddler better known as "Waxey" Gordon.

Gordon controlled the beer business in New Jersey and most of New York City. He was one of the biggest illegal liquor importers on the Atlantic Coast. Gordon, a multimillionaire, owned blocks of real estate in Philadelphia and New York, lived in a castle complete with a moat in southern New Jersey, and owned a fleet of ocean-going rum ships, night clubs, and gambling casinos. In 1928, 1929, and 1930, Gordon paid an average of $33 a year in federal income tax.

By 1931, Waxey Gordon was ripe for elimination. He had feuded with Meyer Lansky, the brains behind the emerging National Crime Syndicate, and at the same time was fighting with Dutch Schultz over control of beer brewing and bottling. Fearing more bad publicity in a time when it was already too much in the spotlight, the syndicate voted not to kill Gordon but to let the government remove him. Through Lansky's brother Jake and others, information and leads about Gordon's sources of income were fed to the Internal Revenue Service.

Gordon soon began to worry. In 1931 he paid $35,000 in taxes, a hugh jump from the $100 he had paid over the previous three years. Irey and the Special Intelligence Unit wanted more. In cooperation with Thomas E. Dewey, who had been appointed interim U.S. attorney for the Southern District of New York in 1933, Irey and his agents put together evidence of Gordon's assets and costs of production. (Breweries, which often fill a city block, are hard to hide.) Based on Irey's accumulation of evidence, Dewey prepared over 1,000 exhibits, called 150 witnesses, and was able to have Waxey Gordon indicted for income tax evasion for 1930 and 1931.

On November 20, 1933, Gordon went on trial before Judge Frank J. Coleman. Dewey charged Gordon with a tax delinquency of $187,834.17 for 1930 and $359,580.91 for 1931. Dewey introduced evidence which showed Gordon renting an apartment for $6,000 a year, a very high rent in the 1930s. Gordon had also paid $36,000 to install a bar in his apartment. He wore $160 suits and $225 tuxedos, and had his choice of two Pierce Arrows, two Lincolns, and a Cadillac to carry him on his errands. He also filled his library with $3,800 worth of books, all magnificently bound and all unread.

The jury took only 40 minutes to convict Waxey Gordon on all counts. In December 1933, he was fined $80,000 and sent to prison for ten years. The special agents from the Internal Revenue Service again did what traditional law enforcement officers were unable to do—they put another major organized crime figure behind bars.

The Special Intelligence Unit did not limit itself to investigating members of organized crime. Irey's domain included any acts of criminal tax evasion, even in some areas where no hint of organization could ever be detected. The Special Intelligence unit's broad investigative responsibilities soon brought it in contact with "Kingfish" Huey Long, the famous Louisiana populist who wanted to be president of the United States. At 21, after completing what normally would have been three years worth of legal training in eight months, Long had become a lawyer. By age 35 he was elected Governor of a mud-covered Louisiana on a campaign promise of "free bridges, free textbooks, and paved roads."

Long proceeded to keep this promise, borrowing and then spending more than $100 million for public works. In the process of spending such a huge sum of money, Long and his organization acquired almost feudalistic control over the state of Louisiana, through control over who received which construction contracts. Money was power and Long had command over who got the money. A great deal of it stuck to his hands and the hands of those who worked for him.

The Louisiana House of Representatives impeached Long on 19 charges, including bribing legislators, fixing the state courts, misappropriating funds, calling out the militia to override the courts, blackmail, and gross personal misconduct. But the Senate never got a chance to convict him.

A two-thirds vote would have been necessary to convict. Fifteen state senators, though, signed a petition stating that they would never vote to convict Long regardless of what he was proven guilty of doing or attempting to do. This was enough to kill any chance for a two-thirds vote and the "Famous Fifteen" soon received great individual political and business plums. Before long, the Internal Revenue Service stepped into the battle against another alleged untouchable.

The Special Intelligence Unit sent 32 agents into Louisiana to uncover evidence of graft, bribes, kickbacks, and the famous Long "deducts" system, under which every state employee had to contribute 2 to 5 percent of his salary to the Democratic Party.

By 1932 Huey Long had bequeathed the governorship to O. K. Allen and had gone on to the United States Senate. Although Allen had the title, Long retained control. Allen's talents and independence were best described by Long's brother Earl, who said that "A leaf once blew in the window of Allen's office and fell on his desk. Allen signed it."

The Special Intelligence Unit examined every contract issued by the State of Louisiana since Long had been elected Governor, and investigated 232 individuals, 42 partnerships, and 122 corporations.

On September 7, 1935, former Texas Governor Dan Moody, who had been recruited as a federal prosecuting attorney in the case by President Roosevelt himself, declared his intention to go before the October Grand Jury and ask for an indictment against Long. But Long would never face formal tax evasion charges or trial. The next day, September 8, Huey Pierce Long was murdered in the Louisiana State Capitol. His alleged assassin, Dr. Carl Weiss, was shot down by Long's bodyguards. Weiss had a .22 caliber pistol in his hand; Long died from a single bullet wound made by a .45 caliber slug.

Long was dead, but plans for the prosecution of his organization continued. The grand jury brought in the necessary indictments but in May 1936, an election year, United

States Attorney Rene A. Viosca refused to prosecute the cases. He called them "weak" and conviction "improbable."

The Treasury Department was furious. Though only Justice could go forward with criminal prosecutions, Treasury decided to bring civil actions against members of the Long organization for payment of taxes due.

The defendants did not even try to refute the Internal Revenue Service evidence. Each indicted member of Long's coalition admitted guilt and paid the assessed taxes plus penalties. Even the estate of Huey P. "Kingfish" Long paid up. Over $2,000,000 in taxes and penalties was collected.

Treasury had won the first battle but the war lasted three more years. By 1939, this time with Justice Department backing, the Special Intelligence Unit had completely broken up the old Long kickback machine and collected for the American public a total of $4,372,360.24 in additional taxes and penalties.

The Long machine in Louisiana was not the only powerful political organization to be challenged by the strong-willed Elmer Irey and his Special Intelligence Unit. In Missouri, another political machine fed and nurtured a man who served in the United States Senate and eventually became president of the United States. Harry S Truman's "mentor," the man to whom he was a faithful and devoted follower, was the head of that machine. His name was Thomas J. Pendergast.

"Boss" Pendergast of Missouri had wanted to play professional baseball. His father, though, would not hear of it. In 1892, at age 20, Thomas Pendergast began a different career: he went to work with his brother Jimmy who owned several Kansas City saloons and controlled a fledgling political organization. Jimmy bought his brother a job as a Kansas City First Ward police officer and the future "Boss" soon learned the superior power of the dollar over the law. In 1911, when Jimmy died, Thomas J. Pendergast took over what was by then a highly organized and professional political machine.

The Pendergast organizational skill refined and perfected Missouri election procedures. In 1936, his First Ward, with a population of only 19,932 (including children), successfully cast 20, 687 votes. Statewide, of 240,000 ballots examined by the FBI, over 18,000 had been altered.

To accomplish this, Pendergast needed more than organizational skill: he needed money. His addiction to the race track, where he would bet $20,000 a day and where in one 31 day period in 1925 he lost more than $600,000, also required a substantial income. Pendergast found it in bribes, kickbacks, prostitution, and massive political tribute from those who owed their position to the "Boss."

Thomas Pendergast made one mistake—he didn't report all this income. In 1935, an insurance company paid him a bribe of $750,000; the Special Intelligence Unit of the Internal Revenue Service was later able to prove this. Charged with an unpaid tax liability of $265,465.15 for 1935 and 1936, Pendergast was indicted for tax evasion and, in May 1939 he pleaded guilty. The "Boss" received a light 15 month sentence, but the Pendergast machine had been cracked. It was soon shattered by indictments of Kansas City's chief of police, director of public works, and city manager. Irey's Internal Revenue Service Intelligence Unit again accomplished what conventional law enforcement agencies had failed to do.

Elmer Irey had begun his Treasury career with a six man Special Intelligence Unit in 1919. When he retired on September 1, 1946, Irey's agency had 1,300 agents, and in 1976 its successor, the Intelligence Division, employed over 2,700 special agents. Six good men with extraordinary powers controlled by an honest, shy leader constituted a manageable, low-risk investment. But when large numbers of investigators are endowed with special powers over the American populace one must scrutinize more closely the need for such intelligence agents and the appropriateness of their association with the Internal Revenue Service.

The 1960s brought to this nation a new or at least different awareness of the role of our government. In the early 1970s this new perspective led to a skepticism and distrust of federal bureaucracy and its omnipresent imposition on our daily lives. Some people, including congressmen, began to question the value of the Internal Revenue Service's law enforcement activities. The growth of the agency's investigative force and role as a national fiscal policeman only led to more skepticism. In December 1975, the U.S. Senate Finance Committee Subcommittee on Administration of the Internal Revenue Code began a formal study of exactly what law enforcement role, if any, the Internal Revenue Service should have.

The subcommittee held hearings in part to air the many views on whether the IRS should assist in federal criminal investigations not involving, or only peripherally involving tax matters. A closely related question was this: If and when the IRS assists in those inquiries, should the agency be permitted to continue to use its special tax collection powers, such as the right to conduct searches and seizures or summon records without court order?

The hearings first investigated the Internal Revenue Service Intelligence Division's involvement in law enforcement. Many witnesses said that only through Internal Revenue Service efforts had any law enforcement agency made real progress against organized crime.

Until President John F. Kennedy appointed Robert Kennedy attorney general, the federal government's efforts to fight organized crime were disorganized, with each agency pursuing a limited mission. In 1961, though, the new attorney general, who had once served as chief counsel to Senator John McClellan's special committee to investigate organized crime, urged government law enforcement agencies to increase and coordinate their efforts against organized crime.

Bobby Kennedy came to the Department of Justice and attacked: "I am tired of hearing people talk about their limited problems. From the citizens' perspective, organized crime is a serious threat; the corruption associated with it is a serious problem. I want somebody to know what the left hand is doing. I want to put general-purpose people concerned with organized crime in the field talking simultaneously with Internal Revenue Service agents, FBI agents, and the Bureau of Narcotics agents, and I want them to look at the whole problem, and not through the limited perspective of special purpose agencies, but from the general perspective of citizens worried about the enforcement of all the federal criminal laws." The IRS responded by establishing an "Organized Crime Drive" within the Intelligence Division.

A study covering the period from 1958 to 1963 concluded that after the IRS established this Organized Crime Drive major racketeers immediately reported 57 percent more average gross income. By the end of the program, the Organized Crime Drive had conducted more than 6,000 tax investigations, resulting in 2,200 convictions and the collection of over $3 million in additional taxes. Fines and other penalties assessed and collected exceeded $300 million.

In response to a May 5, 1966 speech by then President Lyndon Johnson, the Organized Crime Drive was expanded. To quote from the 1966 Internal Revenue Service Report:

In line with the President's directive, the Intelligence Division is now in the process of establishing the Organized Crime Drive as an integral part of regular district operations, thereby making available to the Organized Crime Drive the knowledge and skills of all intelligence division supervisory personnel.

In Executive Order 11396 (February 7, 1968), President Johnson designated the attorney general to coordinate the criminal law enforcement activities of all federal departments and agencies, recognizing that ". . . coordination of all Federal criminal law enforcement activities . . . is desired to achieve more effective results."

In 1968, Attorney General Ramsey Clark tried to coordinate Federal organized crime investigations by creating special inter-agency "Strike Forces" in 18 cities. These Strike Forces focused their attack on illegal sources of income such as gambling, loan sharking, narcotics and prostitution. This naturally required extensive help from the Internal Revenue Service Intelligence Division.

The question of how successful these efforts were was answered before the Senate committee by Charles L. Fishman, Washington counsel for the Federal Criminal Investigators Association. He compiled an eleven year history of statistical information on the Intelligence Division and the Internal Revenue Service's participation in the Organized Crime Drive and Strike Force activity from 1964 to 1974. For simplicity, his analysis was limited to the area of tax fraud.

Each year the Intelligence Division received more than one hundred thousand possible cases of fraud from among the 75 to 80 million returns filed. It made substantial investigations of less than ten thousand and, on the average, recommended prosecutions in approximately two thousand cases a year. Every year approximately 1,250 people were indicted for tax fraud and slightly in excess of one thousand were convicted. Taxes and penalties collected averaged more than $100 million each year. Over the total 11 years, $1,180,-500,000 had been collected at a cost of only $525,700,000, a net gain to the government of $654,800,000.

Tax investigations are time-consuming, especially when they concern organized crime figures and their associates. Customary business records are nonexistent, prospective witnesses are uncooperative, obstructionist tactics are the rule, and audit trails are carefully concealed. Unlike the normal situation, in which investigation occurs soon after the crime, federal tax crimes may have taken place several years before the investigation and, depending on how the case is to be made, the agent may need to track back several years before the actual year of the tax fraud to establish evidence.

Despite these problems, many key Strike Force targets were successfully indicted and prosecuted for tax evasion. The Internal Revenue Service contributed valuable leads and expertise, such as reconstruction of complicated financial transactions. This helped other federal agencies participating in the attack on organized crime to obtain indictments for violations outside the direct jurisdiction of the Internal Revenue Service.

Between 1966 and 1974, a total of 442 Strike Force targets were convicted of tax violations at an average cost of three and one-third person years per conviction. Professor Robert Blakey, director of the Cornell University Organized Crime Institute, commented, "When you look at the prosecutions brought against hard organized crime, the offense that is Number 1 is tax evasion." The initial question facing the Senate committee was whether it was worth it.

In fiscal year 1974 the Internal Revenue Service devoted 1,792 man years to Strike Force and other Justice Department related cases. In fiscal 1975, the Intelligence Division of the Internal Revenue Service screened over 150,000 allegations of fraud—8,730 investigations were completed and 2,760 prosecutions were recommended. This was a massive investment in time and effort. In terms of impact on organized crime, over 60 percent of the racketeering convictions during the 1960s stemmed from Internal Revenue Service intelligence work.

Randolph W. Thrower, commissioner of the Internal Revenue Service from April 1969 to June 1971, said in 1971 that "When one considers the participation of all federal agencies in the program, the Internal Revenue Service now provides substantially more than 50 percent of the manpower committed to battle organized crime."

From the point of view of other law enforcement agencies, the Internal Revenue Service is a very valuable ally, because Congress has granted it unique investigative powers. First, the IRS can require the keeping of books and records with much confidential personal and financial information. Much of this information is then sent to the Internal Revenue Service on tax returns. Failure to provide the information may result in imprisonment. Most of this information would not be compiled if there were no requirement to file income tax returns.

In addition to this access to confidential tax information, the Internal Revenue Service has broad investigatory authority. It may ask questions about other people. It may inspect anyone's business records, go door to door looking for people who have not paid taxes, and it may compel anyone to give testimony or surrender evidence. These powers were given for the sole purpose of enforcing the revenue laws.

In addition, the Internal Revenue Service has a number of extraordinary collection powers, such as the jeopardy and termination assessments. These assessments are sometimes used in an effort to tie up a drug dealer's working capital.

Charles Davenport, formerly project director of the Administrative Conference of the United States (which studied Internal Revenue Service procedures), analyzed for the Senate committee which of these special powers made the Internal Revenue Service so valuable in prosecuting organized and white collar crime. He denied that the confidential information on the tax return rendered the Internal Revenue Service indispensable. While evidence turned up in an investigation may come initially from a tax return, Davenport said that "most adherents of criminal law enforcement would not rest their case on access to tax returns."

Mr. Davenport also ruled out the potential jeopardy and

termination assessment hammerlock as the reason for Justice Department requests for added Internal Revenue Service involvement in criminal law enforcement. He admitted, though, that the Strike Force program against drug merchants might not have been as successful without these exclusive Internal Revenue Service prerogatives.

One reason for the agency's popularity among law enforcement agencies might be the quality of IRS investigators. These agents are usually accountants with substantial experience in applying the tax law to complicated financial transactions. Their skill at unravelling complex financial arrangements makes them very valuable in the battle against modern sophisticated organized crime.

In his testimony before the subcommittee, Deputy Attorney General Harold Tyler, representing the Justice Department, cited this expertise as the main justification for increased IRS participation in organized crime investigations. "It is because of their unique financial expertise and familiarity with complex transactions that the cooperation of Internal Revenue Service personnel has been indispensable to the government's efforts against organized and white collar crime," Tyler said.

Mr. Davenport challenged this argument as a basis for increased or even continued Internal Revenue Service involvement. "After more than 50 years as the envy of the policemen of the Western World, the FBI has been unable to develop the expertise to investigate complex money transactions. Do these hearings and all that surrounds them turn on the FBI's alleged inability to train CPAs to understand financial manipulations? Surely, there must be something more involved."

Davenport suggested that the "something more" pushing the Internal Revenue Service in the direction of increased general law enforcement might be the self-interest and psychological desires of the staff of the Internal Revenue Service Intelligence Division itself.

Davenport said IRS investigative agents prefer the greater glory and romance of battling "real" criminals, extortionists, those who have committed bribery and fraud, to the mundane investigation of a doctor or lawyer who merely underpaid his taxes. Another reason for their preference might be the greater freedom in working hours. Criminal investigations do not begin at 9:00 A.M. and stop at 6:00 P.M. They may require more continuous duty, and surely no one knows better than the investigator himself when to start or stop. Perhaps the vital link in a case might be found with thirty minutes additional surveillance. Surely the investigative agent is not unaware of the potential premium pay or compensatory time off being accrued.

Furthermore, their freedom is enhanced by the fact that Strike Force investigators report to two masters. To the Internal Revenue Service they are working under the leadership of an attorney from the Justice Department. Yet, they do not nominally report to the Department of Justice, and that Department does not really hold itself responsible for them. Working on general criminal cases minimizes their accountability compared to working strictly on tax cases, because instead of having to make two actual reports, these investigative agents often make none. Supervisors in each department—IRS and Justice—think the other department is following the case.

Finally, there is always the bureaucratic desire to grow. Everyone wants to build his own empire and general criminal law enforcement provides a bigger world to conquer.

The motives of the Department of Justice are easier to discern. Besides providing access to the powerful weapons of jeopardy and termination assessments, assigned Internal Revenue Service agents who work on general law enforcement cases are not accounted for on the Justice Department budget. Not only are these specialists provided at no cost to Justice, but there also is no official responsibility. Therefore, if an agent of the Internal Revenue should engage in illegal conduct, it is the Internal Revenue Service, not the Department of Justice, that gets the bad press. The fact that the Justice Department is the sponsor of the work is completely overlooked.

Justice need not provide personnel training; there are no risks. The cost is paid by the Department of Treasury and all arrests and convictions are credited directly to the Strike Forces, which are identified with the Justice Department. For Justice, it is a clear "heads I win, tails you lose" proposition.

Many witnesses at the Senate subcommittee hearings argued that the Internal Revenue Service should limit its activities exclusively to tax collection. The American Bar Association argued for its declaration that the "Internal Revenue Service and its personnel should be limited to functions, responsibilities, and duties which are pertinent to the administration of the Internal Revenue laws."

Donald Bacon, IRS assistant commissioner of compliance, in a 1971 Wall Street Journal article, was quoted as saying that Strike Force investigations take six times as much time as investigations of ordinary taxpayers. For this effort, the Internal Revenue Service obtains criminal tax charges against organized crime figures and corrupt politicians. On a strict dollar return on its investment, though, Internal Revenue Service ex-Commissioner Thrower pointed out that organized crime investigations were "... certainly on the whole less productive in tax collections than other cases."

Donald C. Alexander, then Internal Revenue Service commissioner, argued strongly for a relatively small IRS role in the Strike Force program. He said "... it would be inimical to sound tax administration for the service to overemphasize its involvement in cases concerning individuals suspected of organized criminal activity to the detriment of its other responsibilities."

Commissioner Alexander said the real issue was how best to allocate the limited Internal Revenue Service resources.

Thus his statement was implicitly a request for increased funding. If you, the Congress, want us, the Internal Revenue Service, to continue to put organized crime figures in jail, as well as collect taxes, then give us more money. At no point did Alexander question the fundamental propriety of IRS involvement in the Strike Force program.

Arguing strongly in favor of continuing this involvement was Professor Robert Blakey of Cornell. Professor Blakey said the withdrawal of IRS help would be "a major blow to the ability of the government to bring criminal sanctions to bear on racketeers, and . . . outside of the Federal Government, . . . with the exception of one or two major metropolitan areas, the criminal law in this country is not enforced against organized crime."

Internal Revenue Service Commissioner Alexander disagreed, saying that the nation's battle against organized crime could succeed even without IRS involvement.

But former Internal Revenue Service Commissioner Mortimer M. Caplin agreed with Blakey, saying that ". . . for law enforcement officers, and for large segments of the public, taxation brings to mind one of the Federal Government's most effective means for attacking racketeers and organized crime. At times, it has been the only way the Government is able to catch up with major criminals."

If special investigations and examination programs may be developed for legitimate business and legitimate activities, Caplin asked, why should the Internal Revenue Service not do the same for alleged law violations? The Internal Revenue Service has had a history of special audit programs. For example, in 1976 the Internal Revenue Service set up three special audit target programs: one for tax avoidance and evasion by corporations and corporate officers; another for abuses involving tax shelters such as oil and gas drilling, cattle breeding, real estate, and motion pictures; and a third aimed at improper tax reporting of fund raising by political organizations, candidates and contributions.

Caplin believed that those engaged in illegal pursuits were inclined to follow the same illegal conduct in meeting their tax obligations. "With this in mind, the selection for audit of a high percentage of the tax returns of those engaged in criminal activities not only seems to be a reasonable exercise of administrative discretion, but is also consistent with customary Internal Revenue Service practices and standards."

The Internal Revenue Service's mandate is to enforce Title 26 of the United States Code, which sets out the criminal penalties for failure to file an accurate return and pay the appropriate tax. If a case in which the Internal Revenue Service is cooperating appears to have little potential for a prosecution under Title 26, then Internal Revenue Service personnel should consider ceasing work on that case. The question is not whether the Internal Revenue Service has a law enforcement mission. The Congress has charged the Internal Revenue Service with the responsibility of enforcing the criminal sanctions of the Internal Revenue Code. The Internal Revenue Service must therefore devote some of its investigatory resources to white collar crime, organized crime, and political corruption, because these are potentially fertile fields for developing tax evasion criminal cases which may result in recoveries of tax liabilities and penalties. The question Commissioner Alexander raised during the Senate hearings was whether the Internal Revenue Service might have collected more money for the Treasury by allocating these limited resources elsewhere. He implied this was indeed the case.

The arguments against increased or even continued Internal Revenue Service involvement in general law enforcement went beyond questions of allocating limited resources. Many witnesses raised the fundamental issue of the Internal Revenue Service's role in maintaining citizen trust in the structure and operation of our tax system.

Most taxpayers are not involved in criminal matters. It is

bad enough for these taxpayers to have to assess themselves when they fill out the yearly return and "voluntarily" turn over large portions of their income. Whatever cooperation there is between the tax-paying public and the Internal Revenue Service rests on the image of the IRS as a fair administrator of the inevitable tax laws, not as a criminal prosecutor. If the IRS becomes known for being "out to get" people, for various reasons, many taxpayers will be less likely to cooperate with the IRS in all phases of tax collection.

Sherwin P. Simmons of the American Bar Association Taxation Section told the Senate subcommittee that it is "damaging to the confidence of the public in our tax system for the special enforcement tools of the Internal Revenue Service to be used to achieve a nontax, although highly desirable social goal." He recommended that the Internal Revenue Service not be assigned any duties "completely unrelated to the enforcement of our tax laws." He argued that the IRS should be called into investigations of nontax crimes only when investigation by another law enforcement agency shows a particular criminal activity may have tax consequences. Simmons also said the Bar Association believes the IRS should retain supervision and practical control over its agents at all times. Finally, Simmons recommended that Congress "provide the other federal law enforcement agencies with such resources, manpower, and tools as may be necessary to permit them to discharge their nontax investigations" without calling in the IRS.

S. B. Wolfe, Assistant Internal Revenue Service commissioner for compliance, said that our tax system, which intrudes more deeply and more frequently into the private affairs of more Americans than any other branch of the government, ". . . cannot be administered by an agency which lacks public confidence, and the type of criminal law enforcement activities which are currently being urged on the service will destroy that confidence."

He feared that if the Internal Revenue Service permitted

itself and its employees to become entangled in investigations of nontax-related crimes, public trust in the Internal Revenue Service as the administrator of our tax system would be shattered. This, he said, would severely damage our system of self-assessment and our high level of voluntary compliance with tax authorities.

The Internal Revenue laws were designed for the purposes of collecting revenue and enforcing the *tax* laws of our country, and not for the purpose of enforcing the general criminal laws. Precisely because of the Internal Revenue Service's tax collection responsibilities, the IRS and its agents have been given extraordinary remedies not available to the average law enforcement officer. These extraordinary remedies bypass the normal due process of the law. Misuse or misapplication of these extraordinary remedies might, according to the Federal Administrative Conference, adversely affect "... the reputation of the Service for fair and impartial administration of the tax laws."

Recent history tells of these powers too often being both misapplied and misused. One notorious example was the *Janko* case.

Mr. Janko was reputed to be an aide to a Mr. Workman of St. Louis, a notorious gambler. Mr. Janko, for three consecutive years, took as exemptions his two minor children living with his estranged wife. It was not that the two children were not his nor was it that he did not contribute to their support. It was the fact that he didn't contribute *more* than 50 percent of their support that made his deductions improper.

The tax deficiencies in question were $134 for one year and $264 for each of the other two years. Mr. Janko was criminally indicted for the felony of tax evasion, convicted, and sentenced to 10 years in prison.

The *Janko* case served no real revenue purpose and held the Internal Revenue Service and the United States government up to ridicule. As a consequence of Janko's conviction, it is doubtful that many, if any, similarly situated people, members of gambling rackets, decided to give up their errant ways and file more accurate tax returns.

Senator Haskell was shocked by the story: "You would not see any particularly material tax purpose being served by the Janko case?" He was answered by Mitchell Rogovin, former assistant attorney general, Tax Division, and former chief counsel of the Internal Revenue Service: "None whatsoever, Mr. Chairman."

*Janko* was not an isolated instance. In the *Arcado* case, a notorious alleged hoodlum in Chicago was criminally prosecuted for taking too much depreciation on his automobile, a standard never applied to a normal businessman.

Even Sheldon S. Cohen, another former commissioner of the Internal Revenue Service, was disturbed: "It was a pretty flimsy case. . . . It is like getting the town hoodlum for spitting on the street."

This different standard of prosecutorial judgment again applied in the case of a pimp whose autobiography was widely available and sold.

He was arrested and indicted for failure to file his tax returns, and for evading $427 in income taxes. He was sentenced to three years in jail. The Federal Judge in New York who heard this case commented:

There seems to be some form of distortion that is going on here, an unreality, to bring a matter of this kind into the Federal court, requiring the services of a special practitioner, a judge, a clerk, stenographer, a courtroom and a lengthy, detailed report. Is there not any sense of proportion involved in these matters? What excuse is there for bringing a man up on a Federal charge involving $427.81? Are there not other adequate penalties than the imposition of criminal penalties?

One of the cases I found most disturbing was that of Sharon Willits. On May 24, 1973, Ms. Willits was driving a

1972 Cadillac in Miami, Florida, when she noticed that she was being followed by another car. She pulled over to the curb and stopped; the car following her pulled over behind her and stopped as well but no one got out.

Ms. Willits continued down the road and was followed again. She pulled over a second time and the unmarked car pulled up beside her. One Officer Ahearn of the Miami Police Department emerged from the second car and approached her. He had a full beard and long frizzled hair tied in a pony-tail. He was followed by Officer Mosher. Neither was in uniform.

Officer Ahearn identified himself and asked to see Ms. Willits' driver's license and the registration of the car. The car was registered in the name of Dick Cravero, whom these officers suspected of being a narcotics dealer.

Six weeks before, Officer Ahearn had stopped another vehicle driven by Ms. Willits and checked her license on that occasion. Cravero, who was under police surveillance, had been in the car.

This time, Ms. Willits was arrested on a speeding charge. The police officers took her to the station house, not to the department where they would normally take a speeding violator, but to the narcotics division. They then used the trumped-up charge of speeding to examine her pocketbook.

In her purse certain tablets were discovered. These tablets were never placed in evidence but one witness later testified that chemical analysis had shown they were barbiturates. Ms. Willits had claimed that the pills had been purchased pursuant to a doctor's prescription.

The next morning, May 25, 1973, Officer Ahearn advised Mr. John Zahurak of the Internal Revenue Service that Ms. Willits had been arrested and charged with possession of narcotics. He further advised him that Ms. Willits associated with several persons suspected of dealing in narcotics.

Ms. Willits was not employed. She had filed no income tax returns for 1969, 1970, 1971, or 1972. She had been divorced from her husband, Kenneth E. Willits in June 1972. According to the divorce agreement she was to receive $67.50 alimony and $76.50 in child support for her two children each week. Ms. Willits had received the alimony for five months and then received a settlement of $400 in cash and no further alimony. The child support, though, had continued. Pursuant to the divorce, she had also received the house in which she had lived while married. She sold it in spring 1973 for $2,000 cash with the purchaser assuming the mortgage. Since 1972 and throughout 1973, she had been supported by Dick Cravero, the suspected narcotics dealer.

But the Internal Revenue Service was involved in general law enforcement and surely the friend of a dealer must also be a dealer herself. As a dealer, Ms. Willits must have made a great deal of money, the IRS believed. But she had not filed her required tax returns.

Although the police report indicated that only a few pills had been found in Ms. Willits' purse, Mr. Zahurak computed that she had earned commission income of $60,000 on cocaine sales worth $240,000 during 1973. He recommended that her taxable period for the period January 1, 1973 through May 23, 1973 be terminated. He further determined that a tax of $25,549 should be assessed immediately.

On May 25, 1973 at 3:20 P.M., one day after being arrested for "speeding," *all* of Ms. Willits' cash, and *all* of her other property, were seized to pay the "assessed" tax. By Internal Revenue Service action, Sharon Willits had been deprived of all means of supporting herself and her children. Moreover, it was found by the Fifth Circuit U.S. Court of Appeals, *but not until one year later,* that the seizure procedure, though supposedly a tax, was intended only to "harass and punish Ms. Willits for her association with a suspected dealer in narcotics."

Government attorneys have often argued that one function of the Internal Revenue Service's involvement in general law enforcement, specifically the narcotics program, is to deprive narcotics traffickers of their working capital through the use of the tax system. One must question, though, the real impact on Dick Cravero of the jeopardy and termination assessments made against Ms. Willits.

From a strictly revenue point of view, which, after all, should be the IRS's only concern, this type of program was extremely unproductive. In fiscal 1975, Internal Revenue Service narcotics programs cost about $68 million; the program collected only $38 million. The entire venture probably had no real deterrent effects on the taxpaying public. Prosecution and imprisonment of criminals and drug dealers come as no surprise. Deterrence will come from the prosecution of "normal" citizens—the local doctor, lawyer, banker, bartender, or truck driver who violates the tax law.

In Senate subcommittee discussion of the Internal Revenue Service's general law enforcement activities, the debate was drawn primarily between two groups. First, the top administration of the IRS at the time—people responsible for the entire agency—joined civil libertarians in opposing any increase in IRS general law enforcement. Justice Department representatives and IRS criminal enforcement agents argued the opposite view.

The main question, still unresolved, was whether and how certain special Internal Revenue Service powers should be applied. What might have been acceptable in destroying Al Capone could also be applied to the average American citizen. Or it could be used against political opponents.

# 7/DIRTY TRICKS

It [the state] has taken on a vast mass of new duties and responsibilities; it has spread out its powers until they penetrate to every act of the citizen, however secret; it has begun to throw around its operations the high dignity and impeccability of a state religion; its agents become a separate and superior caste, with authority to bind and loose, and their thumbs in every pot. . . .

H. L. Mencken    1926

The reputation of the Internal Revenue Service has had to withstand several major shocks in the last thirty years. The first scandal, during President Truman's administration, stemmed from allegations that the Internal Revenue Service was fixing tax cases for the rich and politically favored. A widespread investigation followed amidst cries of corruption. Joseph Nunan, commissioner of Internal Revenue at the time, was charged with accepting bribes and was later convicted and sentenced to jail. An assistant attorney general, T. Lamar Caudle, was indicted for his participation in an attempted cover-up, as were several others.

After the subsequent reorganization in the 1950s, the Internal Revenue Service was believed to be honest. It remained relatively free of criticism for many years. However, in the mid-1960s, hearings held by Senator Edward V. Long (D.–Mo.) revealed that the Internal Revenue Service had conducted widespread electronic surveillance. This was one indication of the agency's mania for obtaining detailed information on taxpayers under investigation. What is disturbing, and quite frightening, is that the Internal Revenue Service's "holy quest" for information was all too often not restricted by the protections of our Constitution, nor was it limited merely to gathering "tax" information.

The IRS curtailed its electronic surveillance in response to the disclosures of the Long hearings, but trouble of a different sort was brewing. Another scandal involving a different kind of investigative technique soon made headlines. In March 1975, an informant told several Miami newspapers about an IRS undercover spy operation code-named Operation Leprechaun. A 33-year-old Cuban divorcee with three children, Elsa Suarrez Gutierrez, revealed that the Internal Revenue Service had recruited her as an informant in 1972. She was no rookie at spying. From 1968 to 1975, she had been a paid informant for both the Secret Service and the Drug Enforcement Administration. The Internal Revenue Service paid her to help in a widespread investigation of the sex lives and drinking habits of 30 prominent South Floridians, among them a state attorney involved in the Watergate investigation. Other targets included federal and state judges, several city and county commissioners, politicians, lawyers, and a former assistant U.S. attorney.

Gutierrez received a code name, "Carmen," and was asked to gather personal information about the subjects' private lives and not merely to report any illegal activities. The overall purpose was never made clear to her. She was also told to recruit others to help, which she did.

Gutierrez revealed that she had been promised a life-long pension of $20,000 a year and a home abroad if she could come up with information that would "get" Richard Gerstein, the state attorney of Dade County, Florida.

"They told me, 'Get Gerstein in particular because he's making trouble with his Watergate investigation,' " she said.

She was told to find out about the sexual hangups of her targets, and specifically to get evidence—a nude photograph —showing that a certain Miami lawyer was homosexual.

"It was like a small CIA operation," she commented in an interview. "I was supposed to mingle in local exclusive clubs and bars with these judges and politicians, pick up all the dirt I could, maybe even go to bed with them.

"I never did sleep with anybody or get any good dirt during the three months I was on the job. My contacts told me that the people I was supposed to watch were 'no good,' that one was a homosexual, that others had mistresses."

To make her job easier, Mrs. Gutierrez said, the Internal Revenue Service gave her a car and membership in the Jockey, Palm Bay, and Mutiny Clubs, three of Miami's most exclusive organizations. "I would go to these clubs and try to meet the people I was supposed to be watching," she said. "I didn't have a whole lot of luck.

"They also told me to get involved in politics because that would introduce me to a lot of people."

After trying for three months, she felt that she wanted out. "You know this stuff is why many of us left Cuba under Castro," Gutierrez said later. She recalled that when she told her contact in the IRS she planned to quit, he became vehement and threatened her and her children. She asked for police protection.

Gutierrez produced documents to support her assertions. One document was a letter from the Internal Revenue Service concerning the $2960 allegedly paid to her. Another document appeared to be a receipt indicating that she had shared a safe-deposit box at a Coral Gables bank with a John T. Harrison, whom she named along with a Mr. Thomas Lopez as her chief contacts in the agency.

Local Internal Revenue Service representatives referred all inquiries about Gutierrez's charges to the Washington headquarters. Internal Revenue Service Commission Alexander said that all allegations were being investigated even though the activities had been part of the Justice Department's Strike Forces and had predated his appointment as commissioner. Alexander had promised that as long as he was in charge of the IRS, it would never again behave in that manner.

Soon after Gutierrez made her revelations, a second woman, Elizabeth J. Bettner, disclosed that she too had been a paid informant in Miami for Operation Leprechaun from 1970 to 1973. Her job, she said, had been to gather information on politicians who were suspected of accepting bribes or being involved in narcotic trafficking. At a news conference, Bettner disclosed that she had been one of 25 to 30 persons paid between $100 and $150 a week in expenses. Contradicting Gutierrez, she said the Internal Revenue Service had never ordered her to have sexual relations with the subjects of investigations.

The Internal Revenue Service regional and Washington offices refused to comment on whether Gutierrez had been a paid informant, but did concede the existence of Operation Leprechaun. Both offices denied that sexual behavior or other personal matters had been studied.

Another shocking revelation came a week later, in March 1975. Two men, both paid Internal Revenue Service informants, had burglarized the office of a House of Representatives candidate in November 1972. This was announced by Florida State Attorney Richard Gerstein, who had taken a sworn statement from one of the IRS informants, Nelson Vega. (The other, Roberto Novoa, had died in 1974.)

Vega and Roberto Novoa had been recruited by Elsa Gutierrez, and had broken into candidate Evelio Estrella's office from which they stole a filing cabinet filled with documents. The objective of the burglary itself was never established. But in light of subsequent IRS actions, reporters concluded that the burglary and Operation Leprechaun had been part of the Joint Internal Revenue Service–Justice Department Strike Force investigation of Miami crime.

Lawrence Lilly, a local IRS attorney told Vega, at the time he was subpoenaed by Gerstein, that agency regulations forbid an Internal Revenue Service employee from disclosing without proper authorization any information he might have gleaned. Nevertheless, Vega made a sworn statement the next day in Gerstein's office. Lilly would not comment on his own presence at Gerstein's inquiry. Leon Levine, an Internal Revenue Service spokesman in Washington, said Lilly's appearance came in response to news stories that reported Vega to be an Internal Revenue Service employee. But, stressed Levine, no confidential informants are considered employees, and therefore previous Internal Revenue Service authorization to testify was *not* required.

At this juncture, in spring 1975, the House Ways and Means Investigative Subcommittee scheduled testimony about Operation Leprechaun. Five congressional committees, the Justice Department, Gerstein's office, and the Internal Revenue Service itself would soon join the inquiry.

As the investigations proceeded, a squabble arose between the Internal Revenue Service and the Justice Department regarding the Strike Forces. The Justice Department was trying to determine whether Miami Strike Force Chief Douglas McMillan had been responsible for the methods members of the team there had used. Strike Force officials stated that McMillan had shown a lack of judgment in not keeping the Justice Department informed, but put most of the blame on Internal Revenue Service employees who had been manipulated by their own informants.

Internal Revenue Service Commissioner Donald Alexander responded by saying that IRS special agents did only what Strike Force officials told them to do. He stated that the Justice Department had originally proposed the Strike Forces and still had overall control of them. He complained that his agents had been pressed into duties that went beyond their official role and asked that they be limited to strictly tax-related work.

As the drama continued, McMillan asked for a transfer. He charged the press with "yellow journalism ... printing the uncorroborated ramblings of a few questionable informants." He denied that he or any member of the strike force had ever ordered an investigation into the sex life or drinking habits of anyone.

McMillan told the Justice department that for about a year in 1971–1972 he had received intermittent reports from the Internal Revenue Service agents involved in the "market case," an investigation of a local political figure who had allegedly met with politicians at a produce market in order to influence them. The reports, according to two sources, did include some references to sexual and drinking habits, but also plenty of information relevant to any prosecution of the politicians involved. McMillan did not believe Internal Revenue Service agents had asked the informants to gather such private information, but said that IRS personnel may have been "used" by their own informants.

Such personal information, at times, could be relevant to a tax investigation. It could be used to determine whether a person lives beyond his reported income, is being blackmailed, or is transferring his holdings to a mistress or some other third party. However, plans in another case to entrap a judge for homosexual activities do not seem legitimate. The lack of convictions in the "market case" prosecutions also raises questions about whether the people involved were guilty of anything. Furthermore, federal officials never charged Florida State Attorney Gerstein or any other person on Mrs. Gutierrez's list with any crime!

The next revelation about the Internal Revenue Service was that the agency had operated a secret school to train undercover agents. In special "stress seminars," these agents would be tested with women and liquor to see if they could resist revealing their identities. Classes were held at naval bases in Bainbridge, Maryland, and Yorktown, Virginia, and at several private motels. According to former Internal Revenue Service agents, the government budget provided the liquor and the women were federal employees. A spokesman said the schools began in 1962 and ended in January 1973, but there are scant records to support this ending date.

An Internal Revenue Service spokesman revealed that the agency modeled its anti-drug and anti-liquor conditioning techniques on those used by police department vice squads. This way, its agents could pose as criminals to pursue many crime and tax violation cases. One former IRS employee said several hundred agents had this training. The operation was run on a "need to know" basis, and even highly placed officials outside the intelligence sector of the IRS were not informed.

In one case, the IRS rented part of the Washingtonian Hotel, 20 miles from Washington, supposedly for a "private community group." Agents in training were not told which of the women staying at the hotel were federal employees and which were not. They were told to assimilate into the social atmosphere naturally and not to arouse any suspicions. They were not supposed to disclose their identities even after consuming a great deal of alcohol and being questioned by women in intimate circumstances. They were supposed to stick to their covers even under threats or tortures. One agent, drunk and half-dressed, was found on the highway near the hotel late at night by the Maryland police and picked up. He was incoherent for hours and when finally able to comprehend their queries, he would not disclose his identity. He thought it was part of the test! When he finally relented, they turned him over to the revenue service.

Law enforcement officials in other agencies later said this

school was useless and even laughable. "If I have to teach him not to talk when drunk, then he is not undercover material," one official said.

In 1975, Commissioner Alexander ordered agents to submit the names of their informants so the IRS could confirm that money supposedly paid to them had actually reached them. The agency also wanted to find out whether the informants' actions were legal, and whether the information supplied was worth what the agency had paid. Commissioner Alexander, noting that "the budget item for payments to informers and payments to banks for services was more than $500,000 for the year 1974," ordered that any future payments to informants first be approved by the Internal Revenue Service District Directors.

Six Internal Revenue Service agents were not too pleased with all this. They filed suit in Brooklyn Federal Court, charging that the service was interfering with their investigations into crime by forcing them to reveal the names of their unpaid informants. The agents stated that most of their informants were unpaid anyway, and giving out their names would put their lives in jeopardy, thus cutting the agents off from good sources. Their suit was dismissed. They had no legal case to argue.

In June 1975, the Internal Revenue Service submitted to the Joint Committee on Internal Revenue Taxation a 28 page report of its investigation of its Intelligence Gathering and Retrieval System (IGRS), as well as of Operation Leprechaun. The investigation was conducted by the Internal Security and Internal Audit Divisions in Chicago, Los Angeles, Manhattan, Jacksonville, and Miami, which received special attention because of the allegations in newspaper stories. The report gives a good glimpse of the agency's internal mechanics.

According to the report, the Intelligence Gathering and Retrieval System began in May 1973, and ended in January 1975, when it was suspended by the deputy commissioner.

The system was nationwide and contained a "centralized computer system for indexing intelligence information files and open cases. The system is an index, not a data bank of information; the computer contains the location of information items, not the information itself. The IGRS is completely separate, apart and unrelated to the computerized system for processing tax returns."

In May 1973, IRS management had issued guidelines concerning the types of information that should be indexed. The information "must relate to specific subjects or entities; involve financial transactions with potential tax consequences; or illegal activities which fall into our investigative jurisdiction." Special agents were also to evaluate the value and relevance of the information.

However, the study revealed that in Jacksonville, input sheets were not evaluated before being transmitted to the computer system. Discussions with the employees responsible for indexing the information showed "that they interpreted the instructions to mean that all associates or names appearing in documents should be indexed into the system for whatever use might be made of them. They reasoned that acquaintances, associations, movements of subjects and similar information would be of value in investigations of cases." In the other districts tested, technical personnel were screening the input, but were making different interpretations as to what was meaningful and worth indexing. In all four districts, items were being indexed that were not covered by the guidelines. The background material indexed, especially in the Miami office, was often of little value, but resulted in the inclusion of the names of senators and other public figures because they were mentioned in the same article as the primary subject.

Most of the documents indexed were news articles, but "tax return information, memorandums or reports from special agents, police reports, financial information from public records, information from informants and similar material" were also included. The information indexed concerned both prominent and nonprominent persons.

All four districts indexed social information such as well-known personalities visiting a country club or getting married. Information about sexual and drinking habits was collected only in Jacksonville. There a random test of 66 prominent individuals indexed in the files showed that of the 322 line items pertaining to these individuals, three contained information about sex and seven discussed other social activities.

The report called for clarification of the types of information, especially background information that should be indexed. Reports on sex, drinking, and any activity in which large sums of money were spent (conspicuous consumption) were valuable in investigations "using an indirect method of proof of income." However, a mere catalogue of information about sexual hangups, irrelevant to financial transactions, was useless to the Internal Revenue Service. Yet this was what many items in the files covered.

The second half of the 1975 IRS report to the Joint Committee dealt with Operation Leprechaun specifically. The goal of the inquiry was to discover "the extent of sexual and drinking activity gathered; documentation bearing on questionable or illegal activities employed by informants or Internal Revenue Service agents; and the value to tax administration of the information gathered." In addition, correspondence files were analyzed "to determine the extent of management's monitoring of the intelligence gathering project and to evaluate the effectiveness of management controls over confidential expenditures."

The investigation determined that the code name of Operation Leprechaun was not an official Internal Revenue Service term, though some management officials knew of the term and its meaning. It was just one agent's informal term for referring to his network of confidential informants.

Operation Leprechaun was found to be just one facet of

the Intelligence Gathering and Retrieval System, and not a distinct and separate intelligence entity. It was also part of the Miami Strike Force. The operation contributed only a "small portion" of the information in the Intelligence Gathering and Retrieval System. IRS agent John T. Harrison ran Operation Leprechaun, and most of the 594 confidential documents obtained under his direction contained names of tax case suspects and their associates. Clerical processing of these documents consisted of underlining names in the documents and entering the names in the index. The average document contained ten names. All together, Operation Leprechaun provided about 6,000 individual computer entries of the 160,000 in the entire system.

The report found that Leprechaun had begun during the tense period "of local political and judicial corruption in the Miami area." In a memo dated June 28, 1972, the chief of the Miami Strike Force, Douglas McMillan, estimated that at least half the area's judges and commissioners were corrupt. On March 19, 1975, the former Internal Revenue Service group manager told the IRS investigation under oath that in about May 1972, the Chief of the Jacksonville office of the Internal Revenue Service Intelligence Division had given him a list of 12 to 15 names of individuals suspected of political or judicial corruption and had directed him to initiate case development files immediately. It was his understanding that these names had originally been provided by the chief of the Miami Strike Force. The group manager said he was instructed by his intelligence chief to assign an agent to work only on this project. This agent, John Harrison, would consult directly with the Strike Force chief, and the group manager "would only learn of the activities on a need-to-know basis." The Miami office was also encouraged to suggest more targets for investigation.

The Internal Revenue Service National Office had agreed to fund the project on April 25, 1972. From May 1972 to

January 1974, Operation Leprechaun paid a total of $45,-617.28 to informants. But the special agent assigned to the project had contact with some of these informants both before May 1972, and from January 1974 until January 1975, when the intelligence gathering was suspended.

Harrison had 62 informants, both paid and unpaid, between 1972 and 1975. He said that he chose as targets "potential and suspected tax violators based on the premise that it is unusual to find racketeers and corrupt politicians who report their illegal earnings or bribes. . . ." He said he chose his targets on the basis of: (a) his knowledge of suspected tax violators from his years of experience; (b) his evaluation of information in the files of other law enforcement agencies; (c) his intelligence gathering operation (informants); (d) Miami newspaper articles about organized crime personalities and political corruption.

Files showed that he indeed accumulated a staggering amount of information on hundreds of people and groups. But, the IRS report to Congress said, most of the information on these individuals was gathered because of some "tie-in or association with the principal subjects." Harrison got his information through telephone, personal contacts, and written reports. Newspaper articles, public record information, tax return data, reports from other federal and local police agencies, and so on, were included in the Information Gathering and Retrieval System files on these subjects.

IRS review of the 594 documents revealed that 56 contained specifically tax-related information relating to 67 individuals. About a quarter included references to sexual and/or drinking activities. Seventy of the 135 Leprechaun documents that contained information on sex and drinking activities also contained tax-related information, either specific (20) or general (50). The report disclosed that the information collected on 63 of these 70 subjects "was of little or no value in development of the cases." In the remaining seven cases, information collected was of some aid.

Special Agent Harrison, who had been Mrs. Gutierrez's contact, stated in his affidavit that

I did not give a blanket instruction to all of my confidential informants to go out and seek sexual and drinking habits of suspected tax violators. However when the occasion warranted, I did request one or more informants to obtain the identity of a girl or boyfriend. . . . If the girlfriend was found as having been maintained in an apartment or luxurious manner, I would then request the location of the apartment, amount of rent and determination as to whether the subject was making these payments or any other extraordinary related expenditures. All this information would be valuable in a possible tax investigation. I do not recall ever requesting information concerning sex lives and drinking habits . . . , or any other personal information on anyone that was not related to obtaining information or leads regarding suspected tax evaders or avoiders. All personal information turned in to me that I requested, I consider to have potential value.

Some informants alleged that Harrison had instructed them to get such private data, while others testified to the contrary.

Agent Thomas Lopez, who worked with Harrison, said in his affidavit that he had never said anything to Mrs. Gutierrez "about any alleged sex hangups among public officials; did not tell her to get something on public officials; did not say anything about some public official being a homosexual; and did not give her any instructions concerning the obtaining of any information on public officials."

The IRS report to Congress also revealed that Gutierrez did not quit as she had reported, but had been dismissed by Agent Harrison after he discovered that she was going to leak information to the subjects of the project.

Harrison testified that he had no knowledge of any burglary and said that his files included no mention of it. But the files did reveal that on the date of the burglary, the two IRS informants had been in contact with victim Estrella. In addition a manila envelope in one of Harrison's files contained "originals and copies of reports including itemized receipts, invoices, etc., relating to Estrella's campaign." When shown these documents, Harrison said that they looked familiar, but that he could not swear he recognized them.

Gutierrez had said that she and her family had been threatened, but according to the report, the "confidential informant files, debriefing memorandums, and correspondence files reviewed do not contain any information regarding threats or surveillance of Elsa Gutierrez. Special Agent Harrison stated that he pointed out to Gutierrez that the bad things she planned for others can also be planned for her. However, he unequivocally stated that he never threatened Gutierrez, her children, her dog, or anyone associated with her." He had placed her under surveillance twice while she was working for him. The first time was after he suspected her of transmitting false information; the second was after someone told him that she was planning to report his activities to public officials. Another agent, who had been at the meeting in which Harrison fired her, said that he had not threatened her or acted disrespectfully.

Agent Thomas Lopez stated that he had never promised Gutierrez the $20,000 a year or new identity out of the country that she claimed he had. Agent Harrison said that though he couldn't remember specifically, he may have mentioned that in certain warranted cases the government could relocate and provide a new identity for confidential sources.

As for the country clubs, Internal Revenue Service records showed that the agency had not bought membership cards for Mrs. Gutierrez but that it had reimbursed her for memberships in the Mutiny Club and Playboy Club. Records did not show that she had been reimbursed for her membership in the Jockey Club.

According to the IRS report to Congress, the lack of day to day supervision over Agent Harrison was the major cause of the problems. "The review shows that some of the details concerning questionable activities by informants were not evaluated or acted upon by supervisors or managers. In other instances, informant's notes indicated questionable activities, but when the Special Agent transcribed the informant's handwritten notes to a debriefing memorandum ..., references to questionable activities were omitted."

Harrison also bypassed the formal procedure for paying informants. The manual for IRS agents provides that payments are to be made only after the information is evaluated and found to be worth the payment. Harrison usually paid his informants as soon as he received their information, without evaluating it. In some cases he also gave informants periodic "retainer-like" payments, independent of how much information they had given him.

Some documents referred to in the study showed that district, regional, and national IRS officials had been alerted to serious problems in Operation Leprechaun. A memo from Harrison dated September 13, 1972, reported that he was using some informants he had not even met. These informants were recruited by his other informants. Other memos revealed "that he was using informants to instruct and pay other informants, to conduct surveillance on subjects and on other informants and to make background and public record checks on subjects. He acknowledged that such an arrangement was unorthodox and a risky proposition." In another memo, Harrison stated that he was having trouble with one informant, and that he feared Internal Revenue Service activities might be uncovered.

The IRS report concluded with a promise that some of the material uncovered would be sent to the Justice Department for further investigation and proper handling. The agency's internal inquiry would also continue.

Members of the congressional panels investigating the Internal Revenue Service were not fully satisfied with this report, feeling that it covered up more than it disclosed. For example, the report did not reveal how many top officials of the Internal Revenue Service knew about Operation Leprechaun. And details of the burglary remained controversial and unclear.

The House Government Operations subcommittee and Commissioner Alexander had an angry confrontation after Alexander refused to provide certain documents that the committee wanted. The committee members could not believe that the operation was the isolated work of one special agent, and wanted to see depositions and other material the IRS had gathered in its investigation. Alexander refused to release the documents because, he said, they "contained tax-related information that the agency was forbidden by law to give."

Alexander was threatened with a subpoena by Congressman Benjamin Rosenthal, a New York democrat and head of the subcommittee. If Alexander did not honor it, the committee would charge him with contempt. The commissioner capitulated.

Alexander ultimately admitted that it was a grave error for the Internal Revenue Service to pry into the personal lives of suspected tax violators. In contrast, an Internal Revenue Service assistant regional commissioner for the Southeast, E. J. Vitkus, told the House Ways and Means Committee that the operation was worthwhile and that he had approved the plan. He said that such an operation was not unusual for the Internal Revenue Service, but that the Miami operation was larger than most, because the area was considered a hotbed of political corruption and crime.

When reminded of Alexander's opposing view, Vitkus replied, "If that was his statement, I think it was premature and unfortunate. I can honestly say I do not know of a single instance of abuse that grew out of Leprechaun."

But a few months later, Vitkus complained of pressures put on him to retire. He felt it was because he had not condemned Leprechaun and thus had embarrassed the commissioner. He left the service on March 12, 1976, blaming Alexander for his forced retirement.

The Internal Revenue Service was also investigated by the Oversight Subcommittee of the House Ways and Means Committee. After nine months of study, the subcommittee issued a report in January 1976. In this report, subcommittee Chairman Charles Vanik of Ohio said he believed the Internal Revenue Service had "overreacted" to charges the previous spring that its investigators had acted improperly in setting up Operation Leprechaun. The news reports had led Commissioner Alexander to impose new restrictions on the use of confidential funds and on IRS cooperation with other law enforcement agencies. Vanik said the charges had brought the IRS's collection of tax-related information to a virtual standstill, since they "discouraged informants from imparting information on a paid or voluntary basis and demoralized the Intelligence Division." He said the new rules effectively gave "a free pass to organized crime figures and others seeking to evade the payment of federal taxes."

The subcommittee report disclosed that the Internal Revenue Service Personnel Division in 1975 had "cleared of punishable wrongdoing" the Internal Revenue Service agents involved with Leprechaun. The operation was not, as charged, a probe into the private affairs of prominent individuals in Miami. It was aimed at tax-related information, and Agent John Harrison "was successful in collecting tax-related information which resulted in actual or potential tax claims totaling $57 million."

The report criticized high IRS officials for making public

statements which tended to support unverified allegations and lead the public to make unfavorable conclusions as to Operation Leprechaun. "It now appears that these conclusions were both premature and, at the very least, unfortunate." Vanik also said he found that Operation Leprechaun was exclusively an IRS project under Internal Revenue Service control, not that of the Justice Department's Strike Force.

In January 1977, a year later, a federal grand jury which had been investigating the Internal Revenue Service for 18 months concurred, also clearing the agency of any wrongdoing. The grand jury said it found "no evidence that the civil rights of any taxpayer were violated by any one of the Internal Revenue Service employees carrying out their duties. . . . There was no evidence that the agents involved were gathering information for political purposes."

The grand jury criticized the press for publishing sensational exposés of Operation Leprechaun in early 1975, thereby leading Alexander to restrict intelligence activities. The report specifically mentioned the *Miami News*, the first newspaper to print such stories. In the grand jury's opinion, the newspapers, and especially the *Miami News*, should have been more careful when relying on sources, and should have checked more closely for accuracy as well as credibility. One big problem was the continued use "of the catch phrase 'sex and drinking habits,' which . . . was never clearly defined, except as a convenient label for Leprechaun."

According to the grand jury, the press had also sensationalized allegations that the Internal Revenue Service had used "illegal wiretaps, and had threatened a businessman in order to encourage him to spy on the sex lives of his customers." The grand jury said these claims were not true.

In addition, the grand jury revealed that Chris Sanson, the *Miami News* reporter who was responsible for many of the articles regarding Leprechaun, "had acknowledged in her testimony that she had fraudulently helped to create an Internal Revenue Service document that showed that she was to be audited by the revenue service in retaliation for her reporting." The *Miami News* fired her in April 1975.

Douglas McMillan, the Miami Strike Force chief, was transferred to Washington during the investigations and later cleared of any wrongdoing by the Justice Department's Criminal Division.

The question remains open. We have conflicting congressional committee reports and a grand jury conclusion which rejects specific Internal Revenue Service admissions. Contrary to its past image as the noble federal agency bringing down Goliaths of crime like Al Capone, recent Internal Revenue Service incursions into the field of criminal law enforcement brought it little but bad press, a tarnished reputation, and the beginnings of a great deal of trouble.

# 8/TAX HAVENS

The legal right of a taxpayer to decrease the amount of what otherwise would be his taxes, or altogether avoid them, by means which the law permits, cannot be doubted.

Mr. Justice Sutherland
U.S. Supreme Court
*Gregory* v. *Helvering* (1935)

On the portico of the Internal Revenue Service building in Washington, D.C., these words are chiseled in granite: "Taxes are the price we pay for civilization – Oliver Wendell Holmes." But the price of civilization may be too steep for some, and many try to avoid paying taxes. Though tax *evasion* is illegal, tax *avoidance* under certain conditions is permissible.

Legal tax avoidance often involves setting up a foreign trust in a tax haven, usually the islands in the Atlantic and Caribbean. A trust is a separate taxable entity that can be created by a taxpayer who wants to shelter part of his income. Income foreign trusts earn cannot be taxed by the Internal Revenue Service. Corporations as well as wealthy

131

individuals can set up a foreign firm (or a trust) through which the American parent can shuffle paper and profits, thus avoiding or delaying taxes at home.

Even if one of these firms or trusts is completely owned by Americans, its income from foreign activities cannot be taxed by the IRS until the owners receive the profits through dividends. This way, American owners of a foreign firm can legitimately defer taxes on their foreign income until they actually receive it, at which time they can make sure they're in a lower tax bracket or able to show losses to offset the gains. But foreign trusts can also be used to "launder" income from illegal activities in the United States. Once the cash is passed through a series of foreign trusts, no one can trace its origin and it can be invested in legitimate business activities here. Finally, a company within the United States can set up a foreign trust, borrow money from that trust, or say it did, and then pay such high interest that its tax deductions for interest payments eliminate any U.S. tax liability. If the American company then arranges for its "interest" payments to be passed through several similar "shell" corporations overseas, all owned by the same U.S. firm, the money cannot be traced and can later be reinvested in the United States.

Over 15,000 "local" companies have been chartered in the Bahamas, and there is one bank for every 600 residents —twenty times the U.S. ratio. In the Cayman Islands, U.S. companies have set up at least 14,000 telex numbers to serve as "domiciliary companies." There are only about 13,500 residents in the Caymans.

In the 1960s the Internal Revenue Service launched a major offensive against Americans who were taking illegal advantage of these havens to hide, for example, income from tax collectors or to "launder" money from rackets before it was funneled back into legitimate business enterprises in the U.S. Some of the popular havens for these purposes have been the Cayman Islands, the Bahamas, the

New Hebrides Islands, and Liechtenstein. In hundreds of banks located in these and other havens, accounts are protected by strict secrecy laws.

The IRS attempted to trace unreported investments in the Bahamas and the Caribbean. Government efforts to breach the wall provided by the bank secrecy laws were centered on the Castle Bank and Trust Company offices in the Bahamas and the Cayman Islands. If the government could trace the millions of United States dollars that passed through the offices of this company, federal prosecutors could follow up with a widespread crackdown on the illegal use of other tax havens in such places as Bermuda, Panama, and the Netherlands Antilles.

The Internal Revenue Service set up a special intelligence program, Project Tradewinds, headquartered in Miami. Paid informants were used to obtain the names and amount of investment of Americans in the Bahamas and nearby areas.

The program was vulnerable to criticism because of the means sometimes used to get the information. "We never told the confidential informant how to obtain the information . . . and that was his affair," one agent revealed in a newspaper report. "The information was reliable—that was what was important." But this source could not rule out that the confidential informant might have used bribery, fraud, or burglary to obtain the information that ended up at the Internal Revenue Service.

The big break in the project came on January 15, 1973. H. Michael Wolstencroft, managing director of the Castle Bank in the Bahamas, planned to stay in Miami for the night and asked a friend to arrange a date for him. His friend, Norman Casper, was a paid informant for the Internal Revenue Service, code-named TW24. Casper gleefully arranged a date for the banker with another Internal Revenue Service informant and former police officer, Sybil Kennedy. The banker left his briefcase in the woman's apartment, and using a key she had provided, Casper took the briefcase to the home of an Internal Revenue Service agent where the contents were photographed. The copying was carried out by Internal Revenue Service agent Richard Jaffe, head of the Tradewinds project. The briefcase was returned and for months the banker remained unaware of what had happened.

When the Internal Revenue Service agents sorted through their copies of the contents of the briefcase, they found the names of more than 300 Americans doing business with the Bahamian banks, among them a significant number of names of organized crime figures. Government agents believed that the Castle Banks in the Bahamas and the Cayman Islands, and possibly the Castle Bank in Panama, were all part of a single operation.

The list became the basis for a nationwide investigation known as Project Haven, headquartered in New York. But addresses were needed, so several weeks later IRS informant Casper covertly obtained a telephone index card file from a high official of Castle Bank. The agents began to match names on the list with persons who had secret accounts. The Internal Revenue Service estimated these persons together had failed to report $58 million in taxable income. But two important questions remained: Who was responsible for these tax evasion schemes? Who ran Castle Bank?

The evidence from Wolstencroft's briefcase was a gold mine. But had the evidence been obtained legally? Justice Department officials decided that it had been, and grand juries began investigating in late 1973. Due to the complexities of this jigsaw-puzzle affair, the grand jury progressed slowly and stopped its investigation in 1975. In July 1975, Project Haven agents made plans to transmit material on 284 potential tax violators to the Internal Revenue Service field offices. But other forces were at work to complicate the matter further.

In 1975, IRS Commissioner Alexander had learned of Projects Haven and Tradewinds, through the agency's internal investigation of the allegations against Operation Leprechaun. Alexander became concerned about how the list of names had been obtained, and feared that the evidence might indeed be tainted. He also thought the tax haven projects might be further examples of the Internal Revenue Service's undesirably expanded role in criminal investigations. In August 1975, Project Haven was suspended by an acting Assistant Commissioner, Edward Trainor. This decision was later approved by Commissioner Alexander. The plans to use the evidence Project Haven had obtained were halted as well.

Several IRS agents involved in Project Haven soon charged that Commissioner Alexander's suspension of the intelligence project was a cover-up, since his former law firm, Dinsmore, Shohl, Coates and Deupree, was one of the names on the list. The Project Haven agents thought Alexander discovered that his former firm might be involved sometime between early July, when the leads were about to be investigated, and August 13, the day of the suspension. Two federal grand juries soon began an investigation of Alexander's actions, as did the House Government Operations Subcommittee on Commerce, Consumer, and Monetary Affairs headed by Congressman Ben Rosenthal of New York.

An Internal Revenue Service spokesman testified before the Rosenthal subcommittee that Alexander did not know of the firm's possible connection until *after* the suspension was in effect. The IRS representative reported that Alexander said he had never had any dealings with the Bahamian bank on his own behalf or for any of his clients. He said the commissioner did not know if partners and associates in the firm had done any business with the bank. Partner James Coates said he was puzzled as to why his firm's name was on the list.

In response to the inquiries the Internal Revenue Service cancelled the suspension of Project Haven in October 1975. But control of the project was transferred to the Justice Department and the 250 leads Project Haven had gathered were transmitted to the respective IRS and Justice Department offices for proper handling according to the kind and sufficiency of material gathered.

The grand juries also investigated an allegation that Alexander had once been invited on a boating trip by political figures who wanted him to reduce the tax liability of a convicted felon. He allegedly received this invitation after he became commissioner. Alexander said he had no knowledge of such a trip or invitation, and charged that dissident Internal Revenue Service agents were making false allegations, just as he said they had about his law firm.

But shortly before April 26, 1975, the day the boating trip was to have been made, an informant reported it to the Miami IRS office. Both the Internal Revenue Service and the Federal Bureau of Investigation began investigating the trip. In 1975, the grand jury tried to find out whether Commissioner Alexander had received the invitation and dropped his plans for the trip when he realized that the Internal Revenue Service knew about it.

The White House monitored very closely the grand jury inquiry into the allegations against the Internal Revenue Service Commissioner. But a suspension of Alexander, though considered, was deferred because it might imply prejudice.

The grand jury also investigated Alexander's assertion in testimony before the Rosenthal subcommittee that the decision to suspend Haven was not his, and that he had only agreed with Edwin Trainor, the man who had actually suspended the project. But agency officials later confirmed that Alexander had been present at a meeting discussing the suspension.

Other witnesses charge that when Alexander, then a private lawyer, had represented Proctor and Gamble in a 1972 customs case, he had suggested that the firm violate the law. He was also said to have blocked a tax audit of Senator Joseph Montoya for two years, out of political considerations.

Alexander responded in a news interview by charging that former as well as present Internal Revenue Service employees were trying to discredit him by spreading scandalous rumors. He said these dissident agents disagreed with his views and with his attempts to uncover and eliminate inappropriate IRS activities. Inquiries finally cleared Alexander of any wrongdoing. The Justice Department reported it had found no evidence to support allegations that Alexander had halted the tax-haven investigation to protect clients of his former law firm, or that he had testified falsely before a House committee about that action. In addition, the grand jury that investigated Operation Leprechaun in 1977 mentioned that Alexander had been cleared in the preceding year of any charges regarding Haven.

In the meantime, investigations continued, under Justice Department control. Cono R. Namorato, head of the Justice Department criminal division, ran the operation and decided to give the case against Castle another crack. The Justice Department assigned Bernard Bailor, a trial lawyer, to head the case, and a new grand jury investigation was opened.

The investigators had much more to work with at this stage of the game. For months, agents looked through the records of three banks: Bank of Perrine in Miami (which did business with Castle); the American National Bank and Trust Company of Chicago; and the Irving Trust Company of New York. The agent using a "paper chase" strategy, gathered and analyzed every obtainable record, brokerage account, and similar document in order to spot any criminal transaction.

Diplomatic negotiations were another technique used

in piercing the bank secrecy laws. The U.S. and Switzer-
land had recently concluded a treaty allowing the Internal
Revenue Service to obtain certain financial records "in
exchange for its willingness to help the Swiss trace investments in the U.S." This treaty was implemented under the
direction of Alexander, who several times pointed out that
the Internal Revenue Service did not have to depend on
illegal methods to find the names of citizens with secret
bank accounts. Today, every taxpayer by law is required to
reveal whether he has a foreign bank account. There were
hints from the prime minister of the Bahamas, Lynden
Pindling, that he too might be willing to aid the U.S. in its
investigations of tax violators.

Many observers expected the government's attempted
crackdown on offshore tax evaders to reveal the involvement of prominent and powerful figures. Many film figures
were believed to use the Castle Bank. For example, Tony
Curtis told reporters that he had a bank account there, but
that he had done nothing illegal. While the main goal of
the government's investigation was to discover who owned
and controlled the bank, the growing IRS pressure on the
illegal use of tax havens also affected the legal use of these
accounts for tax avoidance. Marshall Langer, a Miami
lawyer and expert on tax havens, commented, "The use
of foreign tax havens, even though it may not be illegal, is
now considered anti-social." Because of this, he predicted,
"legal tax avoidance through tax havens may become just
as unpopular as illegal tax evasion." IRS knowledge of a
foreign bank account then, and now, invites a complete tax
audit, even if the tax haven is a legal one.

The investigation against Castle continued and indictments arising from the controversial intelligence project
were soon handed down. A San Francisco federal grand
jury issued the first big indictment in October 1975. Harry
Margolies, 55, a tax lawyer from Saratoga, California;
Quentin Breen, a San Francisco lawyer; Ronald Adolphson,

a San Francisco accountant; and the Banco Popular Anti-liano, which had headquarters on the Caribbean island of Aruba, were charged with helping Margolies' clients evade payment of nearly $1.5 million in federal taxes. Prosecutors said the list of clients included a number of prominent California doctors and lawyers, singer Barbara NcNair, and Olympic diver Sammy Lee.

The Justice Department did not, at that point, establish that Margolies' clients knew the financial maneuvers were illegal, but the matter was referred to the Internal Revenue Service for collection of any tax liability owed by these clients. Margolies himself was said to have created several offshore companies that made fictitious loans to some of his clients. The clients would then deduct from their taxes interest payments supposedly made on the loans.

Project Haven Chief Namorato said that this case was not based on the controversial briefcase caper of 1973, but that other upcoming cases would be. He commented, "The briefcase is still a legal time bomb that could explode in the Government's face. Any case that goes to court must avoid any taint from the briefcase pilfering or the Government must be prepared to prove that evidence developed from material found in the briefcase is legally admissible."

In March 1976, Project Haven's investigations led to another major indictment. A federal grand jury charged Burton Kanton, Roger Baskes, Allan Hammerman, and Samuel Zell with conspiring to defraud the United States. All four were Illinois lawyers, the best known of whom was Kanter, an expert on tax havens and offshore investments. The four were charged with an intricate scheme to conceal $700,000 out of the $9.1 million paid for two real estate properties in Reno. According to the indictment, the scheme involved the creation of a trust at the Castle Trust Company of Nassau.

Defendent Kanter denied any illegal actions and declared he was confident that he would be vindicated. "It is my belief that this indictment is part of an effort of the Department of Justice to justify Project Haven," Kanter said. He described the project as an effort to harass people who used what he called "perfectly legal foreign trusts." He also charged that the indictment was part of an effort to attack Commissioner Alexander for his attempt to limit the illegal intelligence activities of the Internal Revenue Service. This indictment's use of the evidence from the briefcase caper would later hurt the government.

The Justice Department suspected Kanter of being a founder of Castle Bank, but had no proof. One of those who was best informed about Castle was Paul Helliwell, a Miami lawyer and bank president whose firm represented Castle in this country. Helliwell also had a long history of association with the American intelligence community. "I can't tell you who owns Castle," he said in a magazine interview. "It's none of my business. I am satisfied that there is no American ownership." He added, "If I knew who owned Castle today, I might be wrong tomorrow morning, because shares in the bank may be transferred without any public record of the transaction." He and government sources did agree that the CIA was not involved in the operation of Castle. Helliwell was less clear on the Mafia's possible involvement.

In January 1977, a Miami grand jury indicted Rogers Baskes, a Chicago lawyer; George Schallman, a Chicago accountant; and Anthony Fields, a Cayman banker, for "conspiring to defraud the Government through a complicated commodities trading scheme that made use of trusts in the Cayman Islands." The scheme reportedly used phony commodity deals to create $2 million in paper losses for two wealthy owners of McDonald's hamburger franchises. The indictment rocked the Mercantile Exchange in Chicago, and there were indications that other similar schemes would soon be uncovered.

But the briefcase caper soon brought down these Haven-related cases, which had already been weakened by admissions that the government had used "informants, burglary, and bribery of foreign officials in an attempt to crack the wall of banking secrecy that is typical in offshore havens like Nassau and Grand Cayman."

The government's cases collapsed in March 1977, during trial of the case against Jack Payner, a wealthy Cleveland resident. Payner was charged with filing a false return in 1972 because he had not acknowledged his foreign bank account. According to the government, Mr. Payner had denied having any interest in any foreign bank account, but had actually owned a Castle Bank account with a balance of at least $100,000. Witnesses also testified that Mr. Payner at one time had $442,000 on deposit at Castle.

However, in a thundering move, Federal Judge John Manos suppressed all Internal Revenue Service evidence, saying that it was based on the illegal search of Wolstencroft's briefcase in 1973 and dismissing government claims that the evidence against Payner had been obtained "independently." In his 29 page opinion, Judge Manos said, "The court concludes that the United States was an active participant in the admittedly criminal conduct in which Casper engaged. The court finds the Government's action in this case was both purposely illegal and an intentional bad faith act of hostility directed at Wolstencroft's reasonable expectation of privacy." Manos declared that "The Internal Revenue Service agents' conduct was outrageous . . . They plotted, schemed, and ultimately acted, knowing that their conduct was illegal."

Norman Casper, who had testified in pretial hearings, was distressed by the decision and said, "It never happened that way. This is very wrong."

Appeals were anticipated. The Internal Revenue Service and Justice Department did not comment on Manos' ruling, but were fearful that the decision, if sustained, would destory the foundation of the Project Haven prosecutions.

Their fears were realized months later. A *New York Post* article published August 24, 1977, reported that the government had quietly ended Project Haven after Judge Manos dealt his fatal blow. Criminal cases supported by evidence illegally obtained could not be successfully prosecuted.

In both the Leprechaun and Haven affairs, the Internal Revenue Service faced the eternal question of whether the ends can justify the means. This issue has been debated repeatedly in terms of legal, ethical, and moral considerations, but current American legal doctrine states clearly that, in general, the government may not use illegal means to enforce the law.

Weak cases are not the only side effect of using informers. Since the informant's pay is based on the quality of his information, he will often exaggerate, especially if he will not have to testify later. In criminal cases, especially those involving drugs, informers are commonly criminals themselves, recruited through the threat of criminal prosecution. Often agents try to keep their snitches out of jail so that they can continue to use them. Thus certain criminals are likely to go unpunished. The Internal Revenue Service's efforts to apprehend tax evaders and tax violators are worthwhile, but the resulting invasions of privacy and other illegalities cannot and must not be tolerated by the public. If the government, the elected and appointed representatives of the American public, must resort to illegalities and Constitutional violations to enforce the law, then perhaps that law, or the government agency that implements it, needs changing.

# 9/POLITICAL ENEMIES

"In a free society, the institutions of government belong to the people. They must never be used against the people."

Richard M. Nixon    August 15, 1973
address to the nation on the Watergate scandal

The original function of the Internal Revenue Service was exclusively to collect taxes. As we have seen, this role has been greatly expanded. The Internal Revenue Service has historically been involved in general law enforcement. It has also been used as a bureaucratic overlord for temporary federal economic controls. For example, in August 1971, Internal Revenue Service agents were responsible for enforcing President Nixon's wage and price controls.

Whether the Internal Revenue Service is collecting taxes, enforcing general laws, or administering economic regulations, the agency must remain impartial if it is to receive the public support it needs in order to do its job. And to be impartial, the IRS must be politically independent. As

143

former Internal Revenue Service Commissioner Donald C. Alexander stated, the agency's first priority must be "to maintain public confidence in the Internal Revenue Service."

If taxpayers lose their faith in the impartiality of the IRS, they will no longer expect fair treatment and will not be as likely to cooperate with federal tax authorities.

If the Internal Revenue Service were to investigate illegal contributions to certain political candidates selected on political grounds, if it were to conduct special audits to harass political enemies of the administration in power, if it were to favor political supporters of that administration, then the United States could face a massive tax revolt. But all these things have happened. It is not surprising that a Harris poll taken in 1973 found that 74 percent of the American people would be sympathetic to a tax strike.

Many "taxpayers" went beyond sympathy. In that same year, *U.S. News & World Report* stated, "A tax-dodging spree, spreading rapidly, is costing the government in Washington at least six billion dollars a year and threatening to get completely out of hand. . . . Tax experts outside the Internal Revenue Service . . . put real losses as high as five times that much, around 30 billion dollars a year."

It has been reported that over ten *million* Americans are refusing to pay their income tax. Of this number over 100,000 have challenged the government directly by making a public protest of their refusal to pay. Former Internal Revenue Service Commissioner Johnnie Walters said of this tax rebellion, "We are heading for trouble. This is a trend, this is frightening, and we must do something about it."

This tax revolt has developed in part as a response to the reported attempts by federal officials to politicize the Internal Revenue Service. Though the revelations of impropriety reached a peak during the Nixon administration, other administrations were also guilty of trying to politicize the IRS.

During the Johnson administration, for example, the Internal Revenue Service selectively pursued its legitimate investigations of some corporations' attempts to take illegal tax deductions for political contributions.

The technique these firms used was simple. Since a corporation could not normally take as a tax deduction contributions paid directly to political candidates, it would instead channel the money to the candidate through an advertising agency or law firm which would give the contributor a receipt "for services rendered." The intermediary would keep enough to pay its own tax bill on this "income earned" and pass the remainder on to the candidate. As an alternative, the corporation could directly pay the candidate's advertising, printing, or other bills as if it had incurred them. Again, the corporation would have a receipt to support a tax deduction. Both techniques were, and are, illegal. In both cases the rest of the taxpaying public unknowingly subsidizes the politician's campaign.

In 1966, the Internal Revenue Service began to investigate the records of several advertising, public relations and law firms suspected of acting as conduits for political contributions illegally taken as tax deductions. Two years later, candidates and corporations had not only not been prosecuted, but had remained publicly unnamed. And the illegal practices persisted.

The *New Republic* reported that during 1968, a presidential election year, the Internal Revenue Service held back almost 1,000 tax contribution swindle cases from the prosecuting arm of the federal government, the Justice Department. Under a Democratic president, the Internal Revenue Service investigations of the New York mayoralty campaign of non-Republican John Lindsay, of the Senate race of Bobby Kennedy, of the Douglas-Percy contest in Illinois, and of the very election of that president, Lyndon Johnson, in 1964, were kept from public view.

Public attention, though, was allowed in California where

the tax affairs of Sanford "Sandy" Weiner were put on record. Sandy Weiner was the California campaign manager for Republican Senator George Murphy, Republican Lieutenant Governor Robert Finch, former Republican mayor of San Francisco, George Christopher, and Republican Congressman Paul N. McCloskey.

While the Internal Revenue Service acknowledged "the possibility of double billings and fictitious invoices" to make campaign contributions appear tax deductible, no formal charges were leveled. Caesar B. Cantu, one of the Internal Revenue Service agents assigned to the California case, explained that IRS officials in Washington had instructed the California investigators to "proceed cautiously because it is a political investigation and sensitive in that there might be political figures involved."

According to the Internal Revenue Service's Director of Public Information at the time, similar "political" investigations were taking place in virtually all of the 58 Internal Revenue Service districts. Yet only the investigation of Weiner, a Republican, was made public. The Johnson administration recognized the Internal Revenue Service's potential as a means of orchestrating political embarrassment. Its value was more in its nonuse, in delay and hesitancy in the application of its investigative powers and discretion.

In 1968, Republican Richard M. Nixon was elected president of the United States. He soon saw that the Internal Revenue Service could be used as something more than a defensive shield for one's political friends: it could be used as an aggressive weapon for attack. The Nixon administration soon made plans to direct Internal Revenue Service efforts against specific individuals, as well as against groups. Political "enemies" would be punished, while political friends would be protected.

White House pressure built up slowly. In early 1970, Internal Revenue Service Commissioner Randolph Thrower was ordered to give sensitive IRS files on the potentially scandalous tax problems of Alabama Governor George Wallace's brother to then Presidential Special Counsel Clark R. Mollenhoff. Mollenhoff had assured Thrower, on the word of White House Chief H. R. Haldeman, that the president himself wanted the records. Mollenhoff got them from Assistant Internal Revenue Service Commissioner Donald W. Bacon. The files, which indicated that Gerald Wallace might have failed to report kickbacks from state liquor sales and federal highway contracts, constituted potentially explosive ammunition in any attempt to remove George Wallace from the 1972 presidential race. Soon after Thrower released the material to the White House, however, and just three weeks before the Alabama primary in which the Nixon campaign had invested $400,000 to defeat Wallace, the Internal Revenue Service file was leaked to columnist Jack Anderson by the late Murray M. Chotiner, then a White House counsel and political pointman for Mr. Nixon. That leak, an unauthorized disclosure of Internal Revenue Service information, constituted a criminal act. It was just a beginning.

During his June 1973, testimony before the Senate Select Committee on Presidential Campaign Activities, former Nixon aide John Dean revealed the extent of the Nixon administration's efforts to use the Internal Revenue Service for partisan political purposes. Dean alleged that he was asked to stimulate audits on several "political opponents" of the White House and to "do something" about audits that were being performed on friends of President Nixon who felt that they were being harassed by the Internal Revenue Service.

In an August 16, 1971, memorandum, Dean outlined how the administration's "Political Enemies Project" would work. The goal of the project, he wrote in that memo, was to "maximize the fact of our incumbency in dealing with persons known to be active in their opposition to our administration. Stated a bit more bluntly—how can we use the available federal machinery to screw our political enemies."

Under the plan, once a White House staff member suggested that one person or another should be given "a hard time," the Political Enemies Project coordinator would "determine what sorts of dealings these individuals have with the federal government and how we can best screw them (e.g. grant availability, federal contracts, litigation, prosecution, etc.)."

Dean suggested limiting the list of enemies to ten names, but the Political Enemies Project staff ignored this recommendation. Instead, the list was frequently updated and expanded to include businessmen, actors and actresses, labor leaders, reporters, senators, representatives, civil rights leaders, McGovern aides, leaders of peace organizations, general "anti-Nixon" people, democratic party contributors, and others. One such list, which Dean said someone on Charles Colson's staff had sent him, contained 205 names. Dean also said that Charles Colson, former Special White House counsel, maintained a special priority list of 20 political enemies. The list, with White House commentary, was as follows:

1. Picker, Arnold M., United Artists Corporation: Top Muskie fundraiser. Success here could be both debilitating and very embarrassing to the Muskie machine. If effort looks promising, both Ruth and David should be programmed and then a follow-through with United Artists.

2. Barkan, Alexandre E., National Director of AFL-CIO's Committee on Political Education: Without a doubt the most powerful political force programmed against us in 1968. ($10 million dollars, 4.6 million votes, 115 million pamphlets, 176,-000 workers—all programmed by Barkan's C.O.P.E.—So says Teddy White in the Making of the President '68). We can expect the same effort this time.

3. Guthman, Ed, Managing Editor L.A. Times: Guthman, former Kennedy aide, was a highly sophisticated hatchetman against us in '68. It is obvious he is the prime mover behind the current Key Biscayne effort. It is time to give him the message.

4. Dane, Maxwell, Doyle, Dane and Bernbach: The top Democratic advertising firm—They destroyed Goldwater in '64. They should be hit hard starting with Dane.

5. Dyson, Charles, Dyson-Kissner Corporation: Dyson and Larry O'Brien were close business associates after '68. Dyson has huge business holdings and is presently deeply involved in the Businessmen's Educational Fund which bankrolls a national radio network of 5 minute programs—Anti-Nixon in character.

6. Stein, Howard, Dreyfus Corporation: Heaviest contributor to McCarthy in '68. If McCarthy goes, will do the same in '72. If not, Lindsay or McGovern will receive the funds.

7. Lowenstein, Allard: Guiding force behind the 18 year old "dump Nixon" vote drive.

8. Halperin, Morton, leading executive at Common Cause: A scandal would be most helpful here.

9. Woodcock, Leonard, UAW: No comments necessary.

10. S. Sterling Munro, Jr., Senator Jackson's AA: We should give him a try. Positive results would stick a pin in Jackson's white hat.

11. Feld, Bernard T., President, Council for Livable World: Heavy far left funding. They will program an "all court press" against us in '72.

12. Davidoff, Sidney: (Mayor) Lindsay's top personal aide: A first class S.O.B., wheeler-dealer and suspected bagman. Positive results would really shake the Lindsay camp and Lindsay's plans to capture youth vote. Davidoff in charge.

13. Conyers, John, Congressman, Detroit: Coming on fast. Emerging as a leading black anti-Nixon spokesman. Has known weakness for white females.

14. Lambert, Samuel M., President, National Education As-

sociation: Has taken us on vis-a-vis federal aid to parochial schools—a '72 issue.

15. Mott, Stewart Rawlings: Nothing but big money for radic-lib candidates.

16. Dellums, Ronald, Congressman, California: Had extensive EMK-Tunney support in his election bid. Success might help in California next year.

17. Schorr, Daniel, Columbia Broadcasting System: A real media enemy.

18. S. Harrison Dogole: President of Globe Security Systems: Fourth largest private detective agency in U.S. Heavy Humphrey contributor. Could program his agency against us.

19. Paul Newman: Radic-Lib causes. Heavy McCarthy involvement '68. Used effectively in nationwide T.V. commercials. '72 involvement certain.

20. McGrory, Mary, Columnist: Daily hate Nixon articles.

According to John Dean these persons were known to have both the desire and the capability of harming the Nixon Administration.

Dean never said any systematic use was made of the White House lists of political opponents. However, he did state that Nixon's chief of staff, H. R. "Bob" Haldeman, had asked him to initiate tax audits on certain individuals and that Charles Colson had requested a tax audit of teamster official Harold Gibbons be initiated. Dean testified that in all but one case he ignored these and similar requests.

The exception was in the case of Robert W. Greene, who had written an unfavorable article on Charles G. "Bebe" Rebozo, a close personal and political friend of President Nixon. The article had appeared in *Newsday*, a Long Island, New York newspaper. Dean testified that he "got instructions that one of the authors of that article should have some problems," but said he had been reluctant to call Johnnie Walters, the commissioner of Internal Revenue, on this matter. John Caulfield, who was on Dean's staff, however, told him that he "had friends in the Internal Revenue Service" and "was able to accomplish an audit on the individual" by sending an anonymous informant's letter.

Dean's reluctance to contact Walters was due to the Internal Revenue Service's reaction to these enemies list requests. Randolph W. Thrower, Nixon's first Internal Revenue Service commissioner, had insisted upon protecting the traditional and legal requirement that the tax laws be applied on a nonpartisan basis. Thrower's integrity laid the foundation for the Internal Revenue Service's administrative resistance to White House pressure.

As early as mid-1970, White House aides began complaining that the Internal Revenue Service was not responsive enough to their demands. So they tried to infiltrate the agency itself, according to Commissioner Thrower's testimony before the Senate Committee on the Judiciary.

Thrower said that during the summer of 1970, Undersecretary of the Treasury Charles Walker had suggested that he appoint John Caulfield, head of security for the president's office, as Director of the Internal Revenue Service Alcohol, Tobacco, and Firearms Division (ATF). Caulfield, a former New York City police detective, was then performing such White House chores as supervising a sporadic surveillance of Senator Edward Kennedy and wiretapping the home of columnist Joseph Kraft.

Though Walker said the president endorsed Caulfield for the job, Thrower refused to appoint him, saying he was not qualified. A few months later, Thrower said, the White House wanted him to appoint Caulfield chief of ATF's Enforcement Branch. And the White House wanted to remove this department from ATF so Caulfield would report directly to Thrower. When Thrower threatened to resign if this plan were adopted, he was told the White House decided to drop the whole matter.

But it didn't. The administration's next candidate for the job was G. Gordon Liddy, then a Treasury Department lawyer. (Later, Liddy went to jail for his role in the Watergate break-in.) Thrower rejected Liddy's nomination as well.

In his testimony, Thrower said he viewed the first Caulfield nomination as the beginning of an attempt to create "a personal police force" within the Internal Revenue Service. Later, he testified that he had tried to meet with the president to complain, but had learned that "the president did not like such conferences." So he expressed his concern to Attorney General John Mitchell, warning that "any suggestion of the introduction of political influence into the Internal Revenue Service would be very damaging to him [the president] and his administration, as well as to the revenue system and the general public interest." Thrower said he next got a call from Nixon's appointments secretary, Dwight Chapin, who reported that Mitchell had passed along Thrower's complaint and that therefore no conference with the president was necessary. "Thereupon," said Thrower, "I submitted my resignation."

President Nixon appointed Johnnie M. Walters to replace Thrower. The new Internal Revenue commissioner was subjected to the same White House pressure and, like Thrower, refused activities as potentially "disastrous for the Internal Revenue Service and for the administration."

On September 11, 1972, Dean summoned Walters to the White House and gave him a list of 579 McGovern contributors and staff members, asking him to have their taxes investigated in a way that would "not cause ripples." With agreement from Treasury Secretary George P. Schultz, Walters did nothing in response to the request. Instead, he sealed the list of names and locked it in his office safe. In his testimony, he indicated that no one had looked at the list other than the secretary and he. He stated further that he did not give anyone any name or names from the list, nor did he ask any Internal Revenue Service employee or official to take any action based on the list. "With absolutely no reservation," Walters said, "the Internal Revenue Service never took any action with respect to this list."

On July 11, 1973, Walters turned the list over to the Joint Committee on Internal Revenue Taxation. On December 20, 1973 the staff of the Joint Committee issued a report stating that it found no evidence that the returns of any persons on the list were screened as a result of White House pressure.

The most brazen attempted use of the tax power by the Nixon White House was its persistent effort to destroy the reputation of Democratic National Chairman Larry O'Brien just before the 1972 election. Not only was O'Brien's phone bugged, but John Ehrlichman, Nixon's top domestic aide, conceded in secret testimony to the Senate Watergate committee: "I wanted them [Internal Revenue Service officials] to turn up something and send him to jail before the election."

Apparently on its own initiative, the Internal Revenue Service began looking into O'Brien's tax status when it learned from its investigation of billionaire Howard Hughes' income taxes in late 1971 or early 1972 that O'Brien had received "fairly substantial amounts of money" from Hughes. O'Brien conceded that Hughes had paid him about $180,000 for public relations work. According to Walters, Ehrlichman asked Secretary Schultz to have the Internal Revenue Service find out whether this money had been properly reported. The Internal Revenue Service found that O'Brien had reported it for the years 1970 and 1971, had paid "a small deficiency," and that "the examinations were closed."

Ehrlichman was angry at the Internal Revenue Service response and insisted that tax agents interview O'Brien again before the election. They did so, reporting no damaging information. When Ehrlichman learned of this, on August 29, 1972, he scolded Walters in a phone call. With Schultz listening in on Walters' line, Ehrlichman told Walters: "I'm goddam tired of your foot dragging tactics." Reported Walters to the Judiciary Committee: "I was offended and very upset. . . . Following the telephone conversation, I told Secretary Schultz that he could have my job any time he wanted it." Though Shultz wanted him to stay, Walters quit on April 30, 1973.

Under trying circumstances, both Thrower and Walters had been able to preserve their independence and integrity. As White House aide Caulfield himself put it in a memo, Republican appointees at the IRS appeared "afraid and unwilling to do anything that could be politically helpful." But the administration was not completely without friends at the Internal Revenue Service.

John Dean testified that John Caulfield had a contact inside the Internal Revenue Service through whom the Administration learned how to initiate audits and to obtain confidential information. Caulfield later testified that his main contact was Vernon "Mike" Acree, formerly assistant commissioner for inspection, a man who was later promoted to commissioner of Customs by a grateful president.

Contrary to instructions from his direct superior, the commissioner of the Internal Revenue Service, Acree personally handled certain enemies list attacks. The case of Robert Greene, who had written the unfavorable story about presidential friend C. G. (Bebe) Rebozo was one instance. Acree was reported to have told White House aide Caulfield that "an anonymous letter" would be the best way to spark an inquiry into *Newsday* Editor Greene's taxes. Acree further assured him that one would be received by the Internal Revenue Service. In fact, though, Greene was not subjected to a federal audit but was audited by the New York State tax authorities after New York and Internal Revenue Service officials exchanged information.

Another Administration friend in the agency was Roger Barth, assistant to the commissioner of the Internal Revenue Service. Barth helped John Ehrlichman and John Dean by bypassing the normal procedures for handling sensitive cases, that is, cases involving members of either house of Congress, entertainers, associates of the president, and some citizens in high tax brackets. Normally, reports on these sensitive cases went through the Internal Revenue Service chain of command to the commissioner, who would then decide, with the secretary of the treasury, which cases should be brought to the president's attention. For example, cases involving the president's personal friends or large contributors were usually considered important enough to bring to the president's attention in order to avoid any embarrassment for the president and the executive branch. (A similar procedure had been followed since the days of the Eisenhower administration.) But Barth, as assistant to the commissioner, called Ehrlichman directly or sometimes Dean to report on these cases. Johnnie Walters testified later that he was unaware of Barth showing or sending sensitive case reports to John Ehrlichman and that this would have been "out of the routine" at the Internal Revenue Service.

Other reports indicate that on occasion White House staff members had tried to ensure that the IRS not harass or otherwise bear down too hard on cases involving "friends." In one case, that of John Wayne, the Internal Revenue Service made a special study to show that the returns of others in the same industry were given at least as much attention as the return of the taxpayer in question. In another case, it is clear that there was a communication from the commissioner of Internal Revenue to a district director and to the agent working on the return regarding a "friend's" return. Thus, even while the commissioner was resisting the strategy of the Political Enemies Project, the Internal Revenue Service administration *was* deeply involved politically in sheltering the president's reputation. Similarly, while the Internal Revenue Service commissioners fought White House interference, many local districts were susceptible to "anonymous" tips and direct orders from highly placed White House aides.

In this area, the agency's performance was generally admirable. But given its vast powers, even one successful political assassination is one too many. Former Governor Warren Hearnes of Missouri was a victim of such an assassination.

Hearnes was a tough, old-style politician who once headed the National Governors Conference. When he endorsed Senator Edmund Muskie of Maine for president in late 1971, there was talk that Hearnes would be nominated as Muskie's running mate. The rumors reached the Nixon White House, which considered Muskie the prime threat to oust President Nixon.

In deepest secrecy, Nixon aide Alexander Butterfield, who later exposed the infamous White House taping system, asked the FBI to dig up some dirt on Hearnes. Butterfield, who handled many similar projects, later told political columnist Jack Anderson that any such assignment probably would have come from White House Chief of Staff H. R. Haldeman or from Nixon himself.

Anderson reported that the White House had demanded not only the FBI dossier on Hearnes but any other damaging information available from the Internal Revenue Service. The bureau, in a confidential wire to agents in the field, stressed the "urgent nature" of the White House request.

Within two weeks, an FBI staff member dispatched a confidential reply to Butterfield. "On December 22, 1971, you requested an up-to-date name check of the records of the Internal Revenue Service concerning Governor Warren Eastman Hearnes of Missouri," it began. The FBI told Butterfield that an "applicant-type investigation" had been conducted on Hearnes in 1969. The investigation report, which the FBI letter indicated Butterfield would receive, alleged that Hearnes had received political contributions from "hoodlum elements in St. Louis."

Muskie's bid for the White House was destroyed by Watergate "dirty tricks," but Hearnes was not forgotten. After

Nixon's reelection, Internal Revenue Service agents walked into Hearnes' office and told him he was under investigation over a few hundred dollars of disputed taxes.

Publicity from the tax probe haunted Hearnes when he ran for a Senate seat in 1976 and lost to Republican John Danforth. When Jack Anderson asked the Internal Revenue Service why Hearnes had been audited, or what finally happened, the agency refused to comment. But in his column, Anderson implied that the Hearnes audit had been politically motivated.

The Nixon administration did not try to use the Internal Revenue Service just to attack enemies; the administration also tried to use access to IRS files to protect friends. In late 1971, Caulfield testified, he pried loose a "back door copy" of the Reverend Billy Graham's audit file, as well as tax information on John Wayne, to determine whether either man was being "harassed." (At the same time, Caulfield obtained tax information on seven more entertainers—Richard Boone, Sammy Davis, Jr., Jerry Lewis, Peter Lawford, Fred MacMurray, Lucille Ball, and Frank Sinatra.) After reviewing the Wayne file, Caulfield concluded that the actor's tax probe was not out of line. But a handwritten note from Dean to Haldeman's man, Larry Higby, was clipped to Graham's tax sheet, asking, "Can we do anything to help?" Haldeman shot it back with his reply: "No—it's already covered." Investigations of the tax affairs of Presidential friend C. G. Rebozo and Nixon's brothers were also subject to White House scrutiny and pressure.

During the 1973 midyear review of the economy hearings before the Joint Economic Committee, Congressman Henry S. Reuss of Wisconsin asked Treasury Secretary George P. Shultz about Internal Revenue Service aid to friends of the President. Reuss charged that the Finance Committee to Reelect the President had been allowed to escape capital gains taxes on the sale of some $20 million worth of appreciated contributed securities, while the IRS looked the other way.

Reuss was distressed to have found that the Treasury Department had held a press conference in which it publicly announced that CREEP was being excused from paying its tax on the huge amounts it made by selling these securities before October 3, 1972. "True, the announcement said that thereafter the Internal Revenue Service intended to fell tax evasion, but that's locking the stable after the horses are gone, because almost all the sales of appreciated securities were made before October 3," he said.

Reuss first noted that CREEP had not paid any taxes due on the sale of the securities in a memo to Shultz dated July 23, 1973. On August 1, 1973, the Nixon Treasury announced CREEP's exemption from paying taxes on security sales before October 3, 1972. The reason for this special tax dispensation was never given.

Reuss was also concerned about the June 1972 Internal Revenue Service ruling which would have permitted use of the $3,000 gift tax exclusions for gifts to more than one campaign committee for the same candidate. The extra committees had been set up for the express purpose of avoiding taxes. Reuss said testimony showed "that the June ruling was procured by political officers in the Treasury over the objection of career people in the Internal Revenue Service."

Schultz's reply could have been made by any taxpayer about much of our tax law. "The law with respect to the taxability of political parties has been unclear for many years."

Yet, as early as March 19, 1965, in the Internal Revenue Service ruling on the *Democratic League of San Francisco*, the formal Internal Revenue policy had been clearly stated that, "unless a political party has received some sort of tax dispensation, the operative presumption must be that its income is subject to taxation."

Though the administration was successful in this instance of taxation favoritism, its overall political strategy for the Internal Revenue Service must be judged a failure: the IRS, for the most part, simply would not cooperate.

In December 1973, the Joint Committee on Internal Revenue Taxation investigated what effect the White House enemies lists had on IRS audits. The committee staff reviewed IRS files on over 700 individuals who had appeared on various lists of political opponents prepared by White House staff.

Between 1968 and 1971, individuals on one list filed 842 returns, of which 187, or 22.2 percent, were audited. Since the White House political opponents were a relatively affluent group—over half earned more than $50,000 a year—it is probably appropriate to compare them with the national statistics for high income people. Internal Revenue Service records show that people with adjusted gross income over $50,000 tend to be audited about 14 percent of the time. Since 22 percent of the returns on this White House enemies list were audited, they appear to have been audited significantly more frequently than random individuals with about the same incomes. A finer breakdown of the national statistics, however, might show that this was not true. There are at least two reasons why people on the White House political opponents list might have been audited more frequently than average: first, they tended to be involved in a wider range of business activities than the average person with the same income; and second, a large proportion of the political opponents in the middle income range were journalists and writers. People in these professions tend to have large deductions for business expenses, and the special audit formulas used between 1968 and 1971 made them more likely than most people in this income range to be chosen by the IRS's computerized audit selection system.

Of the 491 returns of people on this list considered for audit, 425 or 86.6 percent were selected by these special computer systems. Three more were considered in connection with claims or requests for refunds. Seven were considered because of special computerized IRS audit projects, 21 in connection with prior or subsequent year audits, and eighteen in connection with audits of trusts, partnerships, or corporations. In the other cases the committee staff "had satisfied itself that screening was not the result of White House pressure on the Internal Revenue Service."

The staff reported similar findings from its review of a second list of almost 1000 returns filed during 1970 and 1971.

In addition to determining whether an individual on one of the political opponents lists was audited in a particular year, the staff examined the revenue agents' reports and the workpapers of each audit to find out if the audits were conducted with undue strictness or harassment.

In some cases, committee staff found that the agents had been relatively strict, but this was usually motivated by a previous lack of cooperation on the part of the taxpayer. In an equal number of cases the agents had been somewhat lax. Any income tax audit is inconvenient for the taxpayer being audited. However, the staff found no evidence that revenue agents had attempted to increase unnecessarily this inconvenience for people on the political opponents lists.

In short, the committee staff found "absolutely no evidence that audits of people on the political opponents lists were on the average conducted more harshly than normal." Even in audits which press reports had alleged to have been politically motivated, the staff found no evidence that the taxpayer had been "unfairly treated by the Internal Revenue Service because of political views or activities."

The committee investigators also reviewed the collection activities of the Internal Revenue Service concerning people on the lists. Again, no evidence was found that the Internal Revenue Service had been more vigorous than normal in its efforts to collect unpaid taxes from political opponents of the White House. If anything, the opposite was true. Several individuals on the list appeared to pose collection problems for the Internal Revenue Service. The service had been quite lenient in granting extensions to file in many cases, and had not yet attempted to collect taxes from several political opponents who had failed to file returns. In some cases the agency had not even tried to find out why the taxpayer had not filed.

The staff also found no sign that the Internal Revenue Service had been more vigorous than normal in recommending prosecution for tax violations in the cases of political opponents of the White House.

But what about the Nixon "friends" whose files the White House had obtained? Committee investigators said they found the IRS had not given these sensitive cases any visible special treatment, despite White House requests that the agency not bear down too hard on them. One White House "friend" was indicted; in another situation, though, the government did not prosecute a case involving a prominent "friend." The Joint Committee staff summarized this part of its study as follows:

... there are cases on both the friends and enemies lists in which people who probably should have been audited were not audited, in which audits were not done adequately, or in which returns were not filed and no collection activity has been undertaken. Therefore, the Joint Committee staff does not conclude, although it cannot foreclose, that the instances of lenient audits of White House friends were the result of White House pressure on the Internal Revenue Service.

Nixon's lists were only one threat to the impartiality and political independence of the Internal Revenue Service. A second very dangerous effort began within the agency itself.

From 1969 to 1973, the Internal Revenue Service maintained an unusual set of files full of information about radicals and radical groups. If these files had been the basis for a deliberate campaign to use the IRS's special powers to harass political minorities, the result would have been a serious misuse of government power such as one might see in a police state. Fortunately, this never happened, but the fact that the IRS ever put together these files still concerns civil libertarians who recognize the repressive potential of such collections of information.

The events leading to the formation of the IRS Special Services Unit, which maintained these files, date back to September 1968, when the Permanent Investigations Subcommittee of the Senate Government Operations Committee asked the Internal Revenue Service for access to tax information on 22 activist organizations. Assistant IRS Commissioner for Compliance Donald L. Bacon asked the agency's regional commissioners for information on the groups, noting that "National Office officials may be called to testify or produce information concerning them. . . . Most are newsworthy and many are controversial." Top IRS officials were apparently concerned that they might have to defend the agency against charges that it was doing nothing about activist organizations suspected of flaunting or evading the tax laws.

The following year, the same Senate Committee began extensive hearings on Riots, Civil and Criminal Disorders. On June 18, 1969, Jean Powell, a former member of the Black Panther party, testified that during one period the party had received between $50,000 and $100,000 each month and that most of this income had gone directly to the party's officers. Government witnesses noted that the Black Panthers had neither filed federal tax returns nor ever been audited by the Internal Revenue Service. This revelation led Senator Karl Mundt of South Dakota, the ranking Republican on the committee, to accuse the IRS of giving the party and its members "special treatment." The committee also heard evidence that certain other extremist organizations and individuals were evading taxes. Leon Green, an Internal Revenue Service official, asked whether certain of these politically active groups should have their tax exemption revoked.

Following these hearings, on July 1, 1969, Tom Charles Huston, an assistant to the president, telephoned Roger Barth, special assistant to the Internal Revenue Service commissioner, asking what the Internal Revenue Service was doing about "ideological organizations." According to a later memo from Huston to presidential Chief of Staff H. R. Haldeman, the president in fact "had indicated a desire for the Internal Revenue Service to move against leftist organizations taking advantage of tax shelters" in early 1969—several months before the Senate hearings.

In any case, on July 2, 1969, the day after the telephone call from Huston, several IRS officials held a meeting to discuss how the agency should coordinate information on its investigations of "ideological" organizations. The purpose of this special task force was not only to collect taxes, but to collect as well data on each organization's "motives, its activities, its attitudes, its size and its impact on the general public."

"What we are doing," said a memo dated July 29, 1969, "is trying to assemble all information available from within the Internal Revenue Service, from the Federal Bureau of Investigation, from the Department of Defense, from any other federal agency."

This special task force was named the Activist Organizations Committee and, as a unit, began operating on August 5, 1969. For over two years this unit remained an informal, relatively unstructured organization within the Internal Revenue Service Compliance Division. But its function was made clear by White House Aide Huston: "What we cannot do in a courtroom via criminal prosecutions to curtail the ·
activities of some of these groups," he wrote, "the Internal Revenue Service could do by administrative action."

The Nixon Administration knew not only what the task force was doing, but the moral and political implications of it as well. One Nixon aide said, "We do not want the news media to be alerted to what we are attempting to do or how we are operating because the disclosure of such information might embarrass the administration or adversely affect the service operations in this area or those of other federal agencies or congressional committees."

On May 26, 1970, the unit's name was changed to the "Special Service Group" and on February 11, 1972, when the unit was transferred from Compliance to the Collection Division, it became the "Special Service Staff."

At first, the Internal Revenue Service investigations of activist organizations were directed merely toward a stricter enforcement of the tax laws. There is no evidence that the Internal Revenue Service itself had any intent to develop a political intelligence unit.

Minutes of some of the early Special Service Staff organizational meetings suggest that even those involved were unsure of their precise function. At the first organizational meeting, held July 18, 1969, it was decided that the Committee would investigate certain types of organizations. "Some of these," read the minutes,

may be a threat to the security of the United States and one of our principal functions will be to determine the sources of their funds, the names of contributors, whether the contributions given to the organizations have been deducted as charitable contributions, what we can generally find out about the funds of these organizations. . . . Our principal purpose will be to coordinate the activities within the Compliance Division conducting the investigation of the organization.

At the second organizational meeting, held July 29, 1969, it was reiterated that "what we are doing is trying to assemble all information available from within the service, from the FBI, from the Department of Defense, from any other

Federal agency having information, and from any congressional committee having information. This data will be collated, analyzed, and given to the proper functional unit for attention."

While the early minutes do reflect to some degree how the committee planned to do this, they give little guidance on the types of organizations and individuals which would be the targets. In fact, this vagueness characterized the committee's entire history, as the following sampling from its files indicates:

July 8, 1969—The term "ideological organizations" means different things to different people. (Memorandum for File, "Ideological Organizations.")

July 24, 1969—The type of organization in which we are interested may be ideological, militant, subversive, radical, or other, and one of our first problems will be to define and to determine what kind of organization we are interested in. (Memorandum for File, "Activist Organizations Committee.")

September 19, 1970—The identification of organizations and individuals included in the Special Service Group program is without regard to the philosophy or political posture involved; rather, it is directed to the notoriety of the individual or organization and the probability of publicity that might result from their activities and the likelihood that this notoriety would lead to inquiries regarding their tax status. Another important consideration was the degree of probability that the individuals might be deliberately avoiding their tax responsibilities. (Status Report on Special Service Group.)

Though these descriptions of "targeted" groups were vague, the Special Service Staff's general mission was clear. In a September 19, 1970, letter to the White House, Randolph Thrower, then commissioner of Internal Revenue, spelled out the goal:

Recognizing the responsibilities of the Internal Revenue Service to administer taxing statutes without regard to the social or political objectives of individuals or organizations, a decision was made to establish a method of accumulating and disseminating information on all activist groups to insure that the organizations and the leaders of the organizations are complying with the Internal Revenue laws.

The commissioner stated that the Internal Revenue Service recognized its administration of the tax statutes should be evenhanded, except where "activist" groups are concerned. "The sole objective of the Special Service group," he said, "is to provide a greater degree of assurance of maximum compliance with the Internal Revenue laws by those involved in extremist activities and those providing financial support to these activities."

Once a description of the Special Service Staff was added to the Internal Revenue Manual in April 1972, cooperation from other departments of the IRS increased. What this cooperation meant for target organizations is illustrated by a case involving an unidentified underground newspaper, which was the subject of an October 30, 1972, memorandum from one of the district directors to the national office. The memo describes the district director's frustration at trying to find any information at all about the organization that might be used as a basis for Internal Revenue Service action. The newspaper might be liable for a corporate tax return, the writer of the memorandum noted, but would probably not be liable for any corporate income tax since a check of bank transactions showed that expenses about equalled deposits. Having met with very little success in finding tax violations on the part of the organization, the investigation turned to checking the income tax filing records of most of the individuals indentified with the group. This approach was not very fruitful either, because the individuals were mostly students who had very little income and filed in other districts anyway. Although noting that "the 'group' has the reputation of being armed and dangerous," the memorandum concluded with a statement that "the end result would not justify the effort expended" in conducting a full scale audit of all of the individuals associated with the newspaper. Thus, no further action was taken. The fact remains, however, that federal agents had placed the group under surveillance because it was publishing unpopular, antigovernmental views.

By 1973, the Special Service Staff's role was revised to cover an area more in line with the Internal Revenue Service's original function. In a 1973 supplement to Internal Revenue Service Manual, the Special Service Staff role was refined as follows:

[The Special Service Staff] serves as the focal point for information relating to organizations (or related individuals) involved in tax-strike, tax-resister, tax-protester activities, consolidating data and making appropriate dissemination of information relevant to tax enforcement.

But from 1969 to 1973 the Special Service Staff *did* operate to gather political intelligence. During that period the Special Service Staff had four main functions:

(1) It gathered information on organizations and individuals promoting extremist views and philosophies.

(2) Staff members evaluated this information to determine what action, if any, should be taken to assure compliance with federal tax laws.

(3) When more investigation was needed to determine the extent of compliance by extremist individuals and organizations, the Special Service Staff notified the appropriate office and staff members.

(4) Staff members monitored and coordinated field investigations.

The Special Service Staff sent information to the Audit,

Collection, Intelligence, and Alcohol, Tobacco and Firearms Divisions of the Internal Revenue Service, but engaged in no audit or collection activity itself. Nor did it make recommendations about criminal prosecutions. Its recommendations were rather that a certain tax return should be examined by the Audit Division or that the Collection Division should investigate an individual who had not, but apparently should have, filed an income tax return.

The Special Service Staff collected large amounts of information. By June 1972, there were over 9,800 separate files covering over 2,500 organizations and 7,300 individuals. In collecting all this data, the Special Service Staff apparently functioned in what could best be called a "catch-as-catch-can" manner. A file would be established on an individual or organization simply because some member of the Special Service Staff had seen or heard the name somewhere, perhaps in a newspaper article, an FBI report, or a conversation with an elected or administrative official.

In an example of this "catch-as-catch-can" technique the Special Service Staff came up with the name of a prominent conservative newspaper columnist in an FBI report listing some 250 persons arrested at a peace protest in the Midwest. Special Service Staff files were not established on all 250 of the arrested peace protesters, but apparently only on those few whose names "rang a bell" in the minds of Special Service Staff employees. On the list was the name of a protester who coincidentally had a name similar to that of the conservative newspaper columnist. Despite the fact that other information about the people arrested indicated that this particular person was 19 years old and lived half a continent away from the prominent conservative newspaper columnist, a file on this individual was created.

Special Service Staff documents also show that files were opened on the basis of names on lists of contributors to or officers and employees of organizations whose tax returns had been scrutinized. This department's style of operation was best described in a report to the Subcommittee on Constitutional Rights of the Senate Judiciary Committee as "haphazard."

In addition to collecting information on vaguely characterized "individuals or organizations of interest to the staff who were receiving considerable publicity," a Special Service Staff document stated that files were also established on:

1. Individuals or organizations from which high-level inquiries are made from within or without the [Internal Revenue] Service;

2. Case files received from Technical [Exempt Organization Branch] in which the Staff is interested;

3. Individuals for which requests are received from the Department of Justice for tax returns involving national security cases;

4. Any individuals or organizations of interest to the Staff for which inquiries are received from any of their liaison contacts;

5. Individuals appearing in the Department of Justice listing who were involved in incidents of civil disobedience, when the listing shows the date of birth (about one-third of those appearing on the list).

In other words, if somebody in the government noticed your existence, the odds were good that a file would be opened on you. The usefulness of all these files is another issue entirely.

For the first three of its four years of existence, the Special Service Staff made relatively little effort to find out what happened after it analyzed the information it had collected and had sent its recommendations to other IRS offices. One of the main purposes of the *Internal Audit Report* of August 16, 1972, was to find out how the IRS had used the Special Service Staff's 9800 files. This study found that between

August 1969, and June 1972, the Special Service Staff had sent other IRS offices 182 cases, of which 103 had been completed. The IRS had revoked one organization's tax-exempt status and had recommended prosecution of another. Tax returns had been filed by 124 groups, showing tax liabilities of $56,000 and claiming a total of $3,900 in refunds. In addition, audits of these organizations revealed they owed $50,000 more in taxes. Altogether, the revenue produced by Special Service Staff cases during the three years the survey covered did not even pay for the unit's office expenses and salaries. Another study, this one conducted in mid-1973, and covering 1969 to 1973, showed results only slightly better.

A congressional committee staff report found no evidence that investigations instigated by the Special Service Staff were particularly harsh. "Indeed, in some cases the Internal Revenue Service seems to have been more lenient than normal with prominent extremists, perhaps in order to avoid the charge that radicals were being persecuted."

This Judiciary Committee study also found that the Special Services unit had apparently not been coordinated with the Nixon administration's famous enemy lists. No Special Service Staff files had ever been initiated at White House request. And the committee staff reported that "of the 706 individuals listed by the White House as "enemies," only 22 (roughly 3 percent) were also the subjects of Special Service Staff files. Of the 18 organizations listed by the White House as "enemies," 10 were the subjects of Special Service Staff files, most of which were established prior to 1971, when the "enemies lists" were drawn up.

Nevertheless, the fact remains that in every investigation instigated by the Special Service Staff, federal revenue agents singled out a person or group for special attention simply for holding unpopular political views.

The ultimate effect of the Special Service Staff was best described in a December 1974 Staff Report on Political Intelligence in the Internal Revenue Service prepared for the Senate Judiciary Committee's Subcommittee on Constitutional Rights. ". . . . The Special Service Staff's usefulness, such as it was, lay in the fact that the unit had more information about a given subject—political activists—than any other part of the Internal Revenue Service. The information the Special Service Staff accumulated was used to stigmatize, to set a group of individuals and organizations apart as somehow inherently suspect and likely to be in violation of the tax statutes or other laws."

Called before that subcommittee in 1974, Internal Revenue Service Commissioner Donald C. Alexander defended the legality of the establishment of the Special Service Staff by citing sections of the Internal Revenue Code that authorize the Treasury Department to perform investigations and examine documents to find out how much any taxpayer owes. But Subcommittee Chairman Sam Ervin repeatedly reminded Alexander that the Internal Revenue Code is designed to authorize the Internal Revenue Service to inquire into matters relevant to the administration of the tax laws—not to gather data on the political activities and views of a select group of politically active taxpayers. In the discussion that followed, the chairman repeatedly insisted that the collection of information on "ideological, militant, subversive, or radical" individuals and organizations "publicly engaged in the promotion of extremists' views and philosophies" has "little if any justifiable relationship to the administration of the tax laws." Alexander agreed.

On August 9, 1973, the commissioner had abolished the Special Service Staff. He stated then that "political or social views, 'extremist' or otherwise, are irrelevant to taxation." He told reporters that he had become "pretty disgusted" with the operation and had acted to disband it because it had "accumulated too much about too many people." He already was in agreement with Ervin's view that "the creation of a political surveillance unit such as the Special Service Staff was unauthorized by law, unnecessary to the administration of the tax laws, and, at the very least, a waste of the taxpayers' money."

Ervin might have added that political surveillance by the government is likely to terrify and thereby silence dissenters and unpopular minorities. This, in turn, would threaten the basic political freedoms that underlie our system of government.

The White House attempts to use the machinery of the Internal Revenue Service as a political force had, for the most part, failed. These efforts were thwarted by the administration's inability to make three honest and strong Internal Revenue Service Commissioners bend to presidential pressure. The nation was lucky.

The Nixon administration had attempted, in secret, to use federal money and federal power to harass and destroy its critics. As Indiana Congressman John Brademas declared, "The real enemies Americans most fear are those who would subvert the rule of law and the institutions of freedom." On the whole, those working for the Internal Revenue Service had fought these enemies.

Though the administration's efforts to politicize the IRS had failed, their revelation prompted a new public recognition of the dangers of White House political pressure on the Internal Revenue Service. To ensure that nothing similar ever happened again, the Senate Select Committee on Presidential Campaign Activities made four recommendations for new laws to govern the release of IRS information to the White House.

First, the Committee recommended, all White House requests for any IRS information or action should be recorded both by the person making the request and the Internal Revenue Service. And at least once a year, a record of these requests—and the agency's responses—should be disclosed to appropriate congressional oversight committees.

The committee reasoned that this disclosure would discourage White House aides from making improper requests to the Internal Revenue Service, but would permit proper ones to go through. In its report, the committee commented "There is no reason to think that the effective functioning of the White House or the Internal Revenue Service will be impaired by the disclosure of such requests."

Second, the committee recommended that "sensitive case reports" going to the White House and even to the president himself should include only "the name of the person or group in the report and the general nature of the investigation." This way, the White House could have enough information to avoid the embarrassment of appointing someone under investigation to a high post, and the president could know whether any of his aides or intimates are under investigation. The Committee felt that IRS release of basic information about the case would give the president enough, but not too much, information. In its report, the committee commented, "There is no sound policy reason for providing the White House with the details of on-going investigations, and such disclosure could seriously mar the Internal Revenue Service's reputation for impartiality."

Third, the committee recommended that it be a crime for anyone in the Executive Office of the president, including the president, to receive a copy of anyone's income tax return. This recommendation was prompted by cases in which Nixon White House aides asked for and received copies of the tax returns of White House "enemies." That the returns were often sought and used for improper political purposes is clear.

By making receipt, rather than distribution, criminal, the proposed statute would also cover cases in which White House aides obtained the tax returns from another agency, such as a U.S. attorney's office, to which the IRS could legitimately give copies of tax returns.

Congress incorporated these recommendations in the Tax

Reform Act of 1976. That law, to be discussed in chapter 11, should ensure that the Internal Revenue Service will never become the political tool of the party in power that the Nixon administration tried to make it. What was at stake here was the effectiveness of our self-assessment system of taxation. As former Internal Revenue Service Commissioner Johnnie Walters said, "The very base of the democratic way of life and the republican form of government is built on the self assessment tax system. Now if you louse that up, and it was loused up by those people, we don't have a democracy."

# 10/THE IRS VS. CIVIL LIBERTIES

The accumulation of all powers, legislative, executive, and judiciary, in the same hands, whether in one, a few, or many, and whether hereditary, appointed, or elective, may justly be pronounced the very definition of tyranny.

James Madison
The Federalist, No. XLVII

Every American citizen believes his privacy and his freedom of thought are protected by the Bill of Rights. Yet these and other bulwarks of our constitutional system have fallen or been judicially amended to meet the administrative requirements of the Sixteenth Amendment, which gave Congress the power to tax income. The Internal Revenue Service, the nation's number one collection agency, has at times championed prompt payment over legal principle.

For example, most Americans are aware of the Constitutional protection against self-incrimination afforded by the Fifth Amendment. No one "shall be compelled in any criminal case to be witness against himself, nor be deprived of

175

life, liberty, or property without due process of law. . . ." Yet, in spite of this, each taxpayer is required to sign his tax return, according to the Internal Revenue Code "under penalties of perjury. . . ." This potential criminal penalty on its face is inconsistent with the theory of voluntary disclosure of income. Yet it has been judicially upheld.

The history of this part of the code is intriguing. Until 1942, each taxpayer had to submit a statement made under oath before a notary public. However, in that year, the 1939 Code was amended to require instead a written declaration on the return that it was made under penalties of perjury, a felony which, according to another section of the code, was punishable with a fine of $5,000 and a prison term of three years. In other words, as perjury requires a "voluntary violation of an oath" the code was changed to read that the taxpayer made an oath when he signed his return, and, therefore, the penalities for perjury would apply.

The theory under which a taxpayer can be held criminally responsible for a misstatement on a 1040 form is straightforward enough since the disclosure is "voluntary" and since the taxpayer agrees to accept the penalties of perjury in signing the return, he has waived all constitutional immunity. But how "voluntary" really is the disclosure?

Section 7203 of the Internal Revenue Service Code invokes specific sanctions against those who decline to make "voluntary" confessions:

Any person required under this title to pay any estimated tax or tax required by this title or by regulations made under authority thereof to make a return, . . . keep any records, or supply any information, who willfully fails to pay such estimated tax or tax, make such a return, keep such records, or supply such information, at the time or times required by law or regulations, shall, in addition to other penalties provided by law, be guilty of a misdemeanor and upon conviction thereof, shall be fined not more than $10,000, or imprisoned not more than one year, or both, together with the costs of prosecution.

In other words, the taxpayer may be liable for criminal penalties not only if he declines to make his specific "voluntary" confession on his tax return, but possibly even if he merely fails to maintain certain records.

Moreover, the popular conception of the Fifth Amendment is that it has been interpreted by the Supreme Court in *Miranda* v. *State of Arizona* to exclude as criminal evidence any information obtained from a suspect who does not have advice of counsel and who has not been fully warned of his rights. These Miranda warnings, though, apply only to custodial interrogations. Therefore, unless the taxpayer is "substantially in custody," for example, under Internal Revenue Service "duress" (enough duress to convince a jury that the taxpayer's will was overpowered) or he is questioned in private under "suspect conditions," the taxpayer is not entitled to the Miranda protections. So much for the Fifth Amendment and the Internal Revenue Service.

The Fourth Amendment states:

The right of the people to be secure in their persons, houses, papers, and effects against unreasonable search and seizure, shall not be violated, and no Warrants shall be issued but upon probable cause, supported by oath or affirmation, and particularly describing the place to be searched, and the persons or things to be seized.

In other words, no government agent may copy or remove anyone's papers or records unless a proper court has first issued a warrant for their seizure. This warrant must also describe precisely the place to be searched and what will be seized.

That is the law, and its intent is clear. Yet in a hearing

held January 17, 1968 before the Senate Judiciary Committee Subcommittee on Administrative Practice and Procedure, Reuben Lenske, an attorney from Portland, Oregon, testified that the Internal Revenue Service had repeatedly violated this constitutional mandate.

Mr. Lenske was a controversial figure in the Portland area. He was an organizer for the National Lawyers Guild and a member of the United Nations Association, the American Civil Liberties Union, and the Methodist Federation for Social Action. He was also a member of the Committee to Abolish the House Committee on Un-American Activities. Lenske's social views brought him to the attention of the federal officials in Washington.

In 1959 the Internal Revenue Service decided to investigate his taxes for the years of 1945 through 1958. Instead of providing material in response to specific items or categories being questioned, Lenske gave two agents, George Numan and Albert Deschenes, full access to his files. These agents spent months in the small library in Lenske's law office and not once did Lenske fail to deliver any paper or record relating to innumerable transactions that the agents requested. But that was apparently not good enough.

During this period these agents, without once obtaining and serving the constitutionally mandated judicial warrant, took over 400 pages of documents from Reuben Lenske's records. Furthermore, John Brady, one of Lenske's employees, was "recruited" by the Internal Revenue Service to remove more of Lenske's records, have a microfilm made of them, and supply the service with that microfilm. The original documents were never returned to Lenske's files. Instead they were destroyed.

The result of this investigation, which would have been clearly illegal if it occurred in a larceny case, for example, was that Reuben Lenske was charged not merely with tax evasion, but with criminal perjury, or knowingly making a false return. This criminal charge was based upon a finding that in one year he had reported a loss of $9,940.45 but could prove only $9,231.59 of it, a difference of $708.86.

During the Internal Revenue Service investigation of two and a half years, which included interviews with as many as 1,500 people, and the five and a half years of administrative and judicial appeals, Lenske's law practice and his financial foundation were destroyed. The Ninth Circuit Court of Appeals finally vindicated his original tax return when Federal Judge Madden reversed the original conviction. "This court will not place its stamp of approval upon a witch-hunt, a crusade to rid society of unorthodox thinkers and actors by using federal income tax laws and federal courts to put such people in the penitentiary. This court will not be so used." The Fourth Amendment's warrant requirement and the First Amendment's guarantee of freedom of speech and assembly had no impact on the collection procedures used by certain IRS agents, and it took years of expensive litigation before a court ruled that these rights did apply in a tax case.

That leaves us with the Fifth and Fourteenth Amendments' prohibitions against anyone being "deprived of life, liberty, or property without due process of the law." We have already discussed the jeopardy and termination assessments (see chapter 1).

When the Internal Revenue Service seizes a taxpayer's property to cover an assessed deficiency of income, estate, gift, or certain excise taxes, the taxpayer must petition the tax court to redetermine the deficiency or sue for a refund in the court of claims or a federal district court. During this process, the jeopardy taxpayer, unlike the ordinary taxpayer who has been given notice of a deficiency, loses the use of his property. The IRS is generally precluded from selling any of the seized property during the income tax appeal. On the other hand, when the IRS seizes property to cover an assessed deficiency in other taxes, such as employment or wagering taxes, the agency may sell the taxpayer's property *before* he sues for refund in the court of claims or a federal district court. Not only may the taxpayer be deprived of the use of his property "without due process of the law," but in certain cases, it may be disposed of as well. That's the law. It is unnecessarily strict, and no one has ever been able to justify permitting the government to sell a taxpayer's property even before his case can be heard. The procedure amounts to a violation of the citizen's right to due process of law.

The right of privacy has also been found by the Supreme Court to be protected by the penumbra of the Bill of Rights. Yet privacy and the administration of the Internal Revenue Service are by necessity incompatible. The Internal Revenue Service maintains more files on more people than any other agency or entity in the United States. Understandably, these files are a direct result of the Treasury Department's authority, granted by Congress, to "inquire after and concerning all persons ... who may be liable to pay an internal revenue tax."

While the existence of these files is thus required by the nature of the Internal Revenue Service's responsibilities, the assumption that the IRS uses confidential information sent by taxpayers solely for the purpose of collecting taxes has been seriously challenged in recent years. In two executive orders, President Richard Nixon attempted to require the Treasury Department to turn over the tax returns of 3,000,000 farmers to the Department of Agriculture, for "statistical purposes." Government officials acknowledged that similar orders were later issued for other occupational groups. These orders were rescinded only after more than 100 members of Congress cosponsored bills to revoke them and after the Domestic Council on Privacy and then Vice President Gerald Ford made similar recommendations. As the House Judiciary Committee determined in 1974, in its review of the Nixon orders, the constitutional rights of citizens to privacy and to due process of law, and the constitutional privilege against compulsory self-incrimination, are clearly at issue when confidential tax information obtained from the taxpayer under compulsion of law is sought "for purposes not authorized by law."

The startling fact is that the internal revenue statutes and regulations do not prohibit, or even discourage, government employees from rummaging through tax returns en masse or on an individual basis. Under laws then in effect, income tax returns were "public records" open to inspection "upon order of the President and under rules and regulations prescribed by the Secretary (of the Treasury) or his delegate and approved by the President." The returns could also be furnished to tax officials of the states, to the Joint Committee on Internal Revenue Taxation, and to other congressional committees. Since 1957 more than 70 executive orders have permitted inspection of tax returns by various government agencies, including the Federal Trade Commission, the Department of Health, Education, and Welfare, and the Department of Commerce. Since 1933, Congress has passed at least 47 resolutions authorizing committees to obtain and inspect tax returns.

In general, the courts have not tried to prevent the government from using or divulging income tax information, as the discussion of a few cases will illustrate. In the case of *United States* v. *Fruchtman* (1970), a federal court of appeals held that as long as an Internal Revenue Service investigation is within its statutory authority, "there is no prohibition against another department of government having the benefit of information developed in the Internal Revenue Service investigation." In the *United States* v. *Tucker* (1970), a federal court district held that IRS disclosures of tax records to the Federal Bureau of Investigation did not violate the section of the tax code that makes it a misdemeanor and cause for dismissal for any federal officer or employee to divulge, print, or publish "in any manner whatever not provided by law" the amount or source of income, profits, or losses shown in any income tax return. Accordingly, the defendants' motion to suppress the tax records was denied. In *Laughlin* v. *United States* (1972), the appellate court found that the government's disclosure of income tax information to a grand jury was lawful under the tax code and under a Treasury regulation allowing Internal Revenue Service to furnish income tax returns to United States attorneys for use before grand juries, or in litigation in any court if the outcome could affect the government.

In a similar case, *United States* v. *Sapp* (1974), the Government used taxpayers' returns to show why it should obtain records of the taxpayers' financial transactions. While the court characterized the government's conduct as "a shocking and high-handed treatment of taxpayers and a complete evasion of congressional purpose" in prohibiting the disclosure of income tax returns, it also refused to block the government's investigation. The court said that if the attorney general could "adequately explain" why he would not prosecute the officials responsible for disclosure of the returns, the court would permit the government to have the financial records for its investigation. Subsequently the court said it had received a satisfactory explanation from the attorney general.

Clearly the applicable statutes, regulations, executive orders, and court cases provided virtually no restriction upon the power of the executive branch to obtain and use information contained in income tax returns. In 1974, despite the reported excesses of the previous administration, former President Ford expressly broadened his authority to obtain income tax returns for any purpose by instructing the Internal Revenue Service to deliver the tax returns of any person to the president if he personally signed a written request. The president was not required by the order to give a reason for the request, and he could designate a White House employee to inspect the returns, provided that the employee had a presidential commission and was paid at an annual base rate of at least $28,000. With the president's written permission, the designated employee could then disclose information in the returns to persons other than the president. Thus, the president and commissioned employees he designated became free to obtain, inspect, and divulge information in the tax returns of any person, for any purpose, without making any disclosure to the taxpayer, to Congress, or to the courts.

In September 1974, President Ford also proposed formal legislation that would have required the Internal Revenue Service to furnish any return or other tax information to the president and to "such employees of the White House office as the president may designate," but would have restricted government agencies in their efforts to obtain tax return information. The bill did not pass.

In 1928, Justice Louis Brandeis defined the right of privacy as "the right to be let alone—the most comprehensive of rights and the right most valued by civilized man."

Recent Supreme Court cases have affirmed that this constitutional privilege protects certain business records and personal documents containing information about the individual's private life, such as his membership in, or contributions to, political, social, or other private organizations —all of which might be revealed through access to his tax return.

In the Federal Privacy Act, effective December 31, 1974, Congress determined that the right of privacy has been violated by the compilation, use, and dissemination of personal information by government agencies, and that Congress has the right and the duty to regulate these agencies' practices to prevent further harm.

The Privacy Act regulates what personal information can be put in Government files, and prohibits disclosure of any information without the individual's written consent. There are, of course, exceptions and exemptions: confidential information can be disclosed within the agency that has it; to another agency "for a purpose which is compatible with the purpose for which it was collected"; to the Bureau of the Census; under certain conditions, to any governmental jurisdiction "for a civil or criminal law enforcement activity"; to anyone showing "compelling circumstances" affecting the health or safety of an individual; to either House of Congress or any committee or subcommittee of either House; to the General Accounting Office; or pursuant to a court order.

Although the Executive Office of the president is subject to the Privacy Act, the president himself probably is not. Moreover, while income tax returns are not expressly excepted from the statute, certain federal agencies may take the position that the Act does not cover tax information. According to a Senate Committee Report, a law enforcement agency covered by the Act need not secure an individual's permission to obtain his or her file from a non-law enforcement agency, "e.g., FBI access to a tax return."

Furthermore, the constitutional issue of individual privacy is not restricted merely to the dissemination of data, but includes the question of what limits should be placed on the Internal Revenue Service's power to accumulate that data as well.

In an investigation to determine a person's tax liability, the Internal Revenue Service has legal authority "to examine any books, papers, records, or other data which may be relevant or material" to the investigation. This power includes not only the right to examine records in the possession of the taxpayer but also to summon "any person" having possession or custody of records "relating to the business of the person liable for tax" to produce these records and to testify under oath. In cases where the IRS believes that certain transactions have occurred which may have affected the tax liability of some taxpayer, but is unable to determine the specific taxpayer involved, the service can issue a so-called "John Doe" summons, under which the agency requests books and records relating to certain transactions without specifying the name of the taxpayer involved. These administrative summonses served by the Internal Revenue Service may be enforced where necessary by court procedure, including criminal contempt sanctions for refusal.

"John Doe" summonses have traditionally been issued to banks to identify suspected tax-evading depositors. Many summonses, though, demand "records of all transactions with a bank" or "all books, papers, records, and other documents relating to material required to be included in the income tax returns of all clients." These open-ended requests may be mere "fishing expeditions," imposing a heavy cost on the party receiving the summons.

Until recently, the IRS did not have to notify the taxpayer whose business or financial records were being summoned. In addition, in *United States* v. *Miller*, decided on April 21, 1976, the Supreme Court ruled that the taxpayer or other person to whom the records pertain cannot argue that they are protected by the Fourth Amendment against unreasonable searches and seizures.

In the Theodore Turner case, a tax preparer was served with a "John Doe" summons demanding all records concerning all the returns he had prepared. In the Anderson-Clayton case, the Internal Revenue Service used "John Doe" summonses to investigate all of the soybean farmers in Mississippi. In the Humble Oil case, Humble was served with a "John Doe" summons for the records of oil lessors. The Internal Revenue Service wanted to know whether lessors were taking lease bonuses as income in the year in which the lessee abandoned the lease without production. This was not really a question of illegal actions but rather primarily one of using different accounting procedures. It is interesting to note that in this case the Internal Revenue Service admitted that there was no investigation, that there was no intention of beginning an investigation, and that this was merely part of a "data-gathering" research project. This was too much even for the courts. The Fifth Circuit Court refused to enforce the summons.

The Internal Revenue Service maintains that the use of the administrative summons, including the third-party summons, without showing in advance why it is needed, is a necessary tool in conducting many legitimate investigations concerning the proper determination of tax, and has tried to establish certain safeguards for its use. Agents are instructed to obtain information from taxpayers and third parties on a voluntary basis where possible. When a third party summons is served, advance supervisory approval is required. For a John Doe summons, the advance approval needed must be obtained at a high level.

In a November 1975 statement before the tax code subcommittee of the Senate Finance Committee, I commented on the potential effect of the Supreme Court decision which had validated these sweeping "John Doe" summonses:

The broad implications of the Court's decision legitimize "fishing expeditions" that may be merely invasions of the taxpayer's privacy. They depart from established law by authorizing shot-in-the-dark investigations of thousands of transactions, some of them involving possible criminal penalties, without the minimal due process requirements of notice to the unidentified taxpayer under investigation.

One must be very careful, though, to recognize that the Internal Revenue Service powers discussed above have been legislatively granted. Even those powers limiting our First, Fourth, Fifth, and Fourteenth Amendment rights have grown out of congressional statutes, not administrative actions. Two issues arise here. First, should the Internal Revenue Service have these statutory powers which restrict our constitutional guarantees? The courts have allowed these restrictions in lawsuit after lawsuit brought by citizens who challenged the IRS's unique prerogative. The question then, is whether the American citizen wants to support his representative's decision to create these administrative options.

The second question would be how has the IRS applied these special legislatively granted powers. Here, as we have seen in previous chapters, the Internal Revenue Service, with more power over more people than any other government agency in the United States, has all too often allowed this magnified power to be misused by certain Internal Revenue Service agents. United States Senate hearings have established that Internal Revenue Service methods have included defying court orders, illegally picking locks, stealing records, illegally tapping telephones, intercepting and reading personal mail, using hidden microphones to eavesdrop on the private conversations of taxpayers with their lawyers, using undercover agents with assumed identities, sexual entrapment, and other assorted activities which would be clearly illegal if not performed by the IRS. As Internal Revenue Service agent Thomas Mennitt succinctly put it, "I violate laws at all times; it's part of my duties." At one point, Senator Edward V. Long of Missouri was moved to compare the Internal Revenue Service to a "Gestapo preying upon defenseless citizens." The horrors of these Gestapo-like activities are even worse when one realizes that they are often inflicted at random.

In Kansas City, Missouri, a woman nursing her six-month-old baby was subjected to a grueling four hour interrogation by a team of Internal Revenue Service agents. Mrs. Michael Darrak owed no taxes but the IRS wanted to use her to get to her father. She was refused access to her lawyer, even to her telephone, and was held incommunicado, a prisoner in her own home. Internal Revenue Service threatening and bullying traumatized the young woman, and although her father was subsequently found innocent, she had a nervous collapse.

Bank president Gordon W. Warren of Richland, Missouri, was alone in his office when two Internal Revenue Service agents burst in and demanded the records of one of his depositors. "I'll just notify the depositor," Warren said, reaching for his phone. "If you do that," one of the agents told him, "you'll be liable to a $10,000 fine and ten years' imprisonment." That was a direct lie. There was no penalty for informing the depositor.

Attorney Lew M. Warden, Jr. of Oakland, California answered questions about his own tax return satisfactorily but refused an Internal Revenue Service agent's demand for certain files containing confidential information about some of his clients. Several days later Warden received notice that his business deductions for three years had been disallowed and he owed an additional $19,501.14 in back taxes. The IRS seized his bank account, ordered tenants in a cottage he owned to pay their rent to the Internal Revenue Service, and even confiscated his sailboat. Continued Internal Revenue Service harassment took so much time away from Warden's legitimate business that his income dried up. Warden used most of his savings to prepare his tax case for trial. Four days before the trial was scheduled to begin, the Internal Revenue Service suddenly dropped all charges.

Reno P. Varani, a Detroit businessman and former commander of American Legion Post 375, in nearby Southfield, permitted the Internal Revenue Service to examine one company record that showed a proposed stock transfer between two officers of the firm. Varani offered proof that this stock transfer never took place. Nonetheless, the Internal Revenue Service assessed him $70,843.42 on the deal. Varani's actual income for the year in question was only $17,000.

Six years later, the Internal Revenue Service was still pursuing this claim—now in the amount of $91,147.00 as the result of interest added to the "unpaid amount."

Varani refused to pay the claim, suggesting that if the Internal Revenue Service was so sure of its position, it should take him to tax court and prove its case. Instead, the Internal Revenue Service simply assigned more collectors. One of them, Sam Ginsburg, finally swore out a warrant for Varani's arrest, charging assault because the exasperated Varani had written him a letter in which he said, "If you attempt to seize my property through force you will be met with superior force."

Varani was arrested, handcuffed, held, and sent to trial. The judge, before making a full decision or pronouncing sentence in the matter, cancelled Varani's bond, had him thrown in jail, and then ordered him sent to the federal hospital in Springfield, Missouri, for "observation." The judicial order meant Varani could be held in that prison for a full year—without benefit of trial.

Two weeks after he was committed, the prison psychiatrist issued a report in which he found Varani to be "of superior intellect" and said "no rehabilitation is needed," and added that "no further psychiatric examination is necessary." Six weeks later, Varani was still imprisoned. At last report, the case was still unsettled.

Accountant Donald R. Lord of Dedham, Massachusetts, was still in his pajamas when he responded to a Saturday morning knock on his door. Three Internal Revenue Service agents invaded his home and demanded he produce certain corporate records entrusted to him by a Dedham businessman.

"You better cooperate if you expect to stay in business," one of the agents threatened. "Don't make any telephone calls, or you will be subject to prosecution," he lied.

The Internal Revenue Service agents spent the day interrogating Lord, confiscated several boxes of papers, and threatened him with a jail sentence if he resisted.

Later, a neighbor phoned to tell Lord he had been visited by Internal Revenue Service agents asking questions about him. Still later, he found that Internal Revenue Service agents had visited his bank and copied his financial records. His relatives were questioned, including his 88-year-old grandmother.

Lord called his lawyer. His lawyer was then himself examined. The agents even questioned employees of a hospital where the lawyer had undergone surgery six years before.

In this case, the United States District Court found the Internal Revenue Service's "unlawful pressures" against Lord to be perilously close "to extortion." It ruled the seizure of the records from his office absolutely illegal and forbade the Internal Revenue Service to make any further use of them.

In 1967, 1968, and 1969, *Reader's Digest* published three articles by John Barron detailing sixteen Internal Revenue Service agent atrocities. One article, published in September 1968, quoted an official order in which agents were warned that "We will be watching very closely the Revenue Officer who doesn't average at least one levy per week and one seizure per month. . . ." A California memo gave this order: "Levy at once on known sources of income. . . . Seize assets of taxpayers. . . ." In 1967, the Internal Revenue Service tried 880,000 times to seize salaries and property. "The Internal Revenue Service," said Mr. Barron, "can make the most preposterous claim against anyone, then force him to disprove it. It can seize any citizen's home, car, bank account, or paycheck without offering the slightest proof that he . . . owes taxes. At the very least, Congress should require Internal Revenue Service to give a judge some evidence before swallowing up property and salaries."

Barron's accusations were reported again before Senator Long's Committee investigation of Internal Revenue Service practices. The Internal Revenue Service responded by branding these cases as mostly "misleading half-truths." They replied that these agents should have been reported, and that disciplinary action would have been taken, if warranted.

Vincent Connery, President of the National Association of Internal Revenue Employees, defended his agents.

We are well aware of the fact that your Committee has reviewed a number of cases in which Internal Revenue Service employees, while acting as agents of the Internal Revenue Service and the U.S. Government, were accused of disregarding the rights of taxpayers and their representatives. Considering the total number of taxpayer contacts made by Internal Revenue Service employees during the course of a year, such cases, fortunately, represent a very small minority. Equally significant, however, is the fact that the controversial techniques used were ordered, authorized, tolerated, sanctioned, or condoned by responsible Internal Revenue Service management officials. To be perfectly frank, I must say the scuttlebutt in the Internal Revenue Service circles is that many of these incidents occurred as a result of pressures from the Justice Department.

In response to the above statement, Internal Revenue Service Commissioner Sheldon S. Cohen confessed that his management officials were "perhaps not foreseeing enough." Exactly what that was supposed to mean still escapes me.

Furthermore, Mr. Connery accused the Internal Revenue Service administration of creating a "pervasive fear on the part of their employees," destroying morale through "job harassment" and through administrative insistence upon ordering agents "to invade the privacy of citizens" through wiretapping and other methods "beneath the dignity of the type of employment they have had."

Connery reported that the Internal Revenue Service employee himself was sometimes the victim of invasions of privacy. He cited the case of Mr. Brendon J. Hagarty who, while on Internal Revenue Service premises, had been the victim of IRS Inspection Service "bugging" in violation of his Fourth and Fifth Amendment rights.

Connery also described the case of Mr. Walter M. Joiner, an agent who had been demoted and was appealing the decision. Initially, the Internal Revenue Service administration refused to allow Joiner's attorney to interview any Internal Revenue Service employee, even with the employee's consent, unless the lawyer or his client had previously made "a request of the Internal Revenue Service Director, and let him set up the appointment." Furthermore, one of Joiner's own witnesses, himself an employee of the Internal Revenue Service, was compelled to submit to interrogation by the agency even against his will and without the presence of an attorney of the witness' choice.

The above horror stories are told to indicate the true ultimate police power that certain Internal Revenue Service agents have taken upon themselves. Abuse of this enormous power does occur, even though statistically it does not occur "often."

The American taxpayer is supposed to be protected from this kind of action by Section 7214 of the Internal Revenue Code:

any officer or employee of the United States (1) who is guilty of any extortion or willful oppression under color of law; or (2) who knowingly demands other or greater sums than are authorized by law ... shall be dismissed from office or discharged from employment and, upon conviction thereof, shall be fined not more than $10,000, or imprisoned not more than five years or both.

In other words, if an agent or officer of the Internal Revenue Service demands more than is due, he is subject to a possible fine of $10,000 plus a five-year prison sentence. Yet what of the often-imposed gross and unproven tax demands made by way of jeopardy assessments? The exculpatory word is "knowingly." The excessive agent's shield is a simple plea of ignorance. As has been demonstrated above, the deficient and often abominable actions of some agents have too many times gone unpunished because of the need to prove that they were done "knowingly." The word "knowingly" should be changed to "negligently" or, at least, "with gross negligence."

The Internal Revenue Service itself is now clearly aware of this problem and anxiously responds to complaints. If a taxpayer writes in to complain that he has been bullied or treated unfairly, the agent in question will be invited into his superior's office for a long lecture on public relations. He may also receive a call from the Internal Revenue Service's internal police force, the feared Inspection Service. If one agent is the subject of continued complaints in any single year, that agent will probably be taken out of the field and assigned to other duties, or retired.

Like any other bureaucracy, the Internal Revenue Service has its share of statistical "bad apples." The point is that, while power does not corrupt everybody, if it does corrupt some, it is too dangerous to allow without restraints. What is needed, therefore, is the legislative creation of a controlled system of checks and balances to reduce the concentration of power in the Internal Revenue Service administrative audit process.

# 11/AUDIT OF THE IRS AND THE TAX REFORM ACT OF 1976

It will be of little avail to the people that the laws are made by men of their own choice, if the laws be so voluminous that they cannot be read, or so incoherent that they cannot be understood . . . or undergo such incessant change that no man who knows what the law is today can guess what it will be tomorrow.

James Madison
*The Federalist Papers*   1787

The words of such an act as the Income Tax merely dance before my eyes in a meaningless procession: cross-reference to cross-reference, exception upon exception—couched in abstract terms that offer no handle to seize hold of—leave in my mind only a confused sense of some vitally important, but successfully concealed, purport, which it is my duty to extract, but which is within my power, if at all, only after the most inordinate expenditure of time. I know that these monsters are the result of fabulous industry and ingenuity, plugging up this hole and casting out that net against all possible evasion; yet at times I cannot help recalling a saying of William James' about certain passages of Hegel: that they were no doubt written with a passion of rationality; but that one cannot help wondering whether to the reader they have any significance save that the words are strung together with syntactical correctness.

Judge Learned Hand

194

One fundamental question underlies the history and current operations, both private and public, of the IRS: has this institution and the procedures that are a part of it been effective in protecting taxpayers against abuse and unwarranted tax assessments?

In June 1973 the Joint Committee on Internal Revenue Taxation asked Congress' investigative arm, the General Accounting Office (GAO), to audit the Internal Revenue Service to find out whether the tax code was being administered "fairly" for all citizens. The GAO's findings comprise the first in-depth study of the Internal Revenue Service by any government audit agency.

The General Accounting Office concluded that the "procedures for selecting individual income tax returns for audit generally protect U.S. taxpayers against abuse" but that the "Internal Revenue Service needs to take steps to improve its audit plans and to make sure that the plans are followed." The GAO failed to define clearly what should be contained in the IRS audit plans or what steps should be taken to monitor plan implementation.

The General Accounting Office investigation found no evidence of a formal "quota" system but did note that the Internal Revenue Service's annual plan called for a specific number of audits. Some examiners told the outside investigators that they felt pressure to complete audits and that this pressure was preventing them from doing a quality job. While a collection "quota" did not exist, some auditors clearly felt the effects of a quota system.

The General Accounting Office study found that taxpayers audited by the service centers rather than the district officers were more likely to understand why their returns had been amended, were more likely to have prepared their own returns, and had smaller tax increases but more changes in their returns. The reason for this was that the IRS usually selected these returns because of clearly unallowable items that could often be identified and resolved by mail.

Furthermore, the General Accounting Office found that these returns were usually selected on the basis of defined criteria which minimized the role of personal judgment. Whenever the IRS had to decide which returns to audit, the decision was usually made by someone other than the person who was to perform the audit.

The General Accounting Office did conclude that when an individual service center employee made the selections, taxpayers who overpaid their taxes were less likely to be reviewed. Service center computers were also biased against the overpayer.

The General Accounting Office found relatively more discretion and subjectivity in the district office agents' decisions. Still, most audited returns had been chosen because of their computerized "Discriminant Function" (DIF) score. The GAO found that the DIF system minimized the potential for abuse in choosing returns for audit, since the selection was done not by the examiner who would audit the return, but by a classifier working with a computer. The General Accounting Office did recommend further Internal Revenue Service study to measure how much influence the classifier could exert.

At the district offices, the federal auditors found that examiners could sometimes request returns for audit without having to explain why they needed them or what they eventually did with them. An examiner could audit anyone he chose, when he chose, and if he acted out of spite or for political reasons, no one else would ever know. The GAO proposed a regulation requiring examiners to explain, in writing, why they wanted any return. The explanation for each request would go in the affected taxpayer's file. This, the GAO hoped, would deter any unjustified requests and leave behind a clear record for future review.

The Central Accounting Office study revealed that in order to justify its request for more examiners in 1974, the Internal Revenue Service committed itself to additional audits and tax assessments. Then to carry out these commitments, the Internal Revenue Service deviated from its plan and conducted more audits of medium-income taxpayers—historically the best compliers and generally the easiest returns to audit—and conducted fewer audits of taxpayer classes in which compliance levels were lower.

Still taxpayers in the four districts sampled by the GAO generally praised the way the Internal Revenue Service treated them and conducted its audits. Seventy-two percent of the sample believed the Internal Revenue Service had given them the benefit of the doubt or treated them fairly, while 21 percent felt the Internal Revenue Service had little regard for their position. Taxpayers' feelings about their audits were influenced by the effort required to gather documentation and the size of the resulting tax change.

The taxpayers who agreed to all or part of the tax change but who did not understand the need for the change (58 percent of the sample) usually (1) had no experience in preparing their own tax returns, (2) said they had not been advised or did not remember whether they had been advised of their appeal rights, or (3) considered the effort needed to gather documentation for the audit unreasonable. Most taxpayers (80 percent) agreed to the district office audit findings before they received what is known as a "30-day letter," informing them that they have 30 days to agree with the findings or initiate an appeal.

While the General Accounting Office was preparing its report on the Internal Revenue Service, another government agency, the Administrative Conference of the United States, was recommending adjustments to audit procedures. Congress had created this agency in 1964, to "study the efficiency, adequacy, and fairness of the administrative procedures used by administrative agencies." The conference consists of an eleven-member council, the chiefs of 35 government departments and agencies, and 35 private citizens, including lawyers and professors.

In December 1975 the Conference made several recommendations for changes in IRS administrative procedures. Administrative Conference recommendations do not carry the weight of law and the Internal Revenue Service need not go along with them. But most government agencies usually give serious consideration to any suggestion from the conference. Besides recommending that an agent who requests a taxpayer's file must explain, in writing, why he wants it, as had the GAO, the conference also suggested that when a taxpayer is notified he will be audited, he should receive a brief written statement of the selection program or other criterion by which his return was chosen. The conference urged the Internal Revenue Service to publish statistics each year showing the number of returns examined, the results of the examinations, and other pertinent information, for each of its selection programs and criteria. At a minimum, the conference recommended, the IRS should maintain procedures by which the reasons for the audit selection could be verified for appropriateness and accuracy by an independent oversight committee.

Responding to criticism of the Internal Revenue Service for inconsistent enforcement of the laws in different districts, the conference suggested that the Internal Revenue Service publish a comparative study, for each taxpayer class, of District and Appellate Conference settlements on the issues that arise most frequently. The study would include a comparison and analysis of the recovery ratio—how much the Internal Revenue Service accepted compared to what was originally demanded—as well as the amount of tax involved, whether the taxpayers had professional representation, and any patterns of geographic variation.

The conference report also recommended that when a taxpayer asks for tax law advice from the IRS Taxpayer Service Division, he should be informed that the advice is based on the facts as the IRS representative understands them, and the agency is not bound by it. Finally, the conference proposed that the IRS establish regular procedures to deal with taxpayer complaints and that these procedures be "well publicized and easily accessible to taxpayers through all Internal Revenue Service personnel."

While the GAO and Administrative Conference were investigating IRS procedure, Congress was preparing the first major overhaul of the tax code in years.

The book was paperback and was the color of deep Mediterranean waters on a bright sunny day. It would almost invite reading if it were not for its title, "The Joint Senate-House Conference Comparison of H.R. 10612" and its tabletop size, 12 inches by 16 inches. Its purpose was to summarize and simplify the Tax Reform Act of 1976, but after spending a whole weekend trying to understand its two and one-half pounds of anything but poetic prose I had serious doubts as to its success.

This 133-page "simplified" summary, though, was far easier to read than the actual Act itself, a five and one-half pound, 1,730-page document. Congress had written it in response to public demand for an uncomplicated, straightforward, and readable tax law that could be understood even by taxpayers who had not passed the CPA exam or spent three years studying taxation in law school. The Tax Reform Act was intended to clarify the nation's tax code which, until then, had been understood completely by perhaps one man, its primary author, former Chairman of the House Ways and Means Committee, Wilbur Mills. I have often wondered whether it was the code that eventually drove Mills to drink, to his Tidal Basin encounter with stripper Fanne Foxe, and eventually out of Washington.

As for its goal of creating tax clarity, tax practioners have dubbed the 1976 law the "Attorney's and Accountants Relief Act of 1976." The Act created such confusion, instituted such complexity, and developed so many new formula traps for the tax unwary that innumerable calls were quickly made to professional tax advisors for the necessary guidance and revisions in tax planning. Gift and estate tax changes alone made almost all wills then in effect obsolete. Therefore, they all had to be rewritten.

Changes in the rules on alimony, moving expenses, child care, credits for the elderly, tax shelters, employee benefit plans, and capital gain and loss computations affected every American taxpayer. Reform Act corporate and individual tax amendments left not one taxpayer untouched. Bailing clients out of loopholes lost and jumping them through new ones kept many accountants and lawyers chained to their desks throughout many dark nights dreaming of the happy sound of cash registers ringing.

Most of the Reform Act, if not unintelligible to the professional, is clearly unfathomable to the layman. Even most tax professionals lack a clear understanding of the applicability and meaning of many of the complex provisions of the Act. Even more disturbing, many Internal Revenue Service employees are also unsure of the correct interpretation of many sections. As this book was written, almost two years after passage of the Act, the intellectual mandarins of the Internal Revenue Service bureaucracy were still composing new regulations to explain, interpret, and expound upon a law originally written to "simplify and reform" the original code. The Code and The Reform Act were both enacted by lawyers, speaking to lawyers. It should surprise no one that the language they used was arcane legalese, which creates a greater demand for tax law advice to be billed at rates that can exceed $200 an hour.

One of the main goals of the Reform Act was to reduce the allegedly excessive powers of Internal Revenue Service agents, thereby preventing them from committing the civil and moral injustices they had in the past. The Nixon administration's attempts to misuse confidential individual tax returns had been a major reason for the Privacy Act of 1974. Though that Act put new restrictions on any government agency's disclosure of an individual's records it did not focus specifically on how IRS agents were to handle individual tax returns. The Tax Reform Act of 1976 did.

The Reform Act provided that tax returns and related information are confidential and cannot be disclosed to other federal or state agencies or employees except in certain limited cases. Not just the return itself was covered. So were the taxpayer's identity, his sources of income, his expenses, and, perhaps most important, any other information the IRS had about the return—including information on actual or possible investigations of the taxpayer. Reputations and careers could no longer be ruined with impunity by rumors or reports of pending tax inquiries.

The Reform Act severely restricts the release of tax returns and related information to the White House and other federal agencies. Disclosure is permitted in only two cases: to the president, if he personally signs a written request stating specifically why he wants the information; or, again upon the president's written request, to any named White House employee, or the head of a particular federal agency, identified in the president's request, only for a limited tax check on prospective appointees, and only after notifying that prospective appointee that a tax check is being made.

The maximum penalty for unauthorized disclosure of any return or other tax information was increased from a $1,000 fine and one year in jail to a $5,000 fine and five years imprisonment. Unauthorized disclosure also became a felony instead of a misdemeanor.

The Reform Act of 1976 attempted to strengthen the privacy shield again in its treatment of third-party summonses. A third party summons commands a third party—an attorney, accountant, bank, credit union, stock broker, or the like—give the IRS records regarding a taxpayer under investigation. The third party himself need not be under investigation and, until Congress passed the Reform Act, the taxpayer whose records were being scrutinized and whose dealings were being probed was not even informed that the summons had been served. The Internal Revenue Service could invade your private bank records, interrogate the accountant who had prepared your returns, or study any documents you had given him under an expectation of confidentiality—all without your knowledge, and without a court order. These are administrative summonses, available in a pile in any Internal Revenue Service Office. An agent simply picks forms up and puts them in his briefcase. When appropriate, he pulls one out, fills it in, and hands it to the third party. The summons form says in large type across the top "SUMMONS" and warns that "failure to comply will subject you to proceedings in the district court . . . to punish default or disobedience." The frightened, unsophisticated recipient is terrorized into opening up all of his books and records immediately. If the taxpayer whose records are being summoned makes a "good faith" objection, there must be a court hearing. But to make the objection, he must know of the summons first.

The Reform Act modified this situation by requiring that, if the summons identifies a specific taxpayer, he must receive notice within three days after the summons is served on the third party. This notice need not be delivered personally: leaving it at the taxpayer's home or last known address is sufficient. Moreover, no notice is required if the purpose of the inquiry is to learn the identity of the person maintaining a numbered bank account. Nor must notice be given if a federal court agrees that this might lead the taxpayer to try to conceal, alter, or destroy the records in question; to intimidate, bribe, or conspire with others to prevent the communication of information; or to flee to avoid prosecution, testifying, or production of the records.

The Reform Act also granted the taxpayer the right to participate in any proceeding for the enforcement of the summons. Furthermore, he was given the right to delay compliance with the summons if, within 14 days after notice was given, he asks the third party, in writing, not to comply with the summons and mails a copy of this request to the Internal Revenue Service. The IRS must then wait 14 days before examining the records in question. Thus the taxpayer is given a two week period during which he may attempt to block the third party summons in court.

The federal courts predicted this provision would lead to 38,000 new lawsuits a year, all filed by taxpayers trying to block Internal Revenue Service investigators from obtaining data from banks, brokers, accountants, and credit card companies. But the law provides that the Internal Revenue Service may investigate and inquire after *"all* persons . . . who *may* be liable to pay *any* internal revenue tax . . ." and authorizes the agency to summon witnesses and examine books and financial records that may be relevant for "ascertaining the correctness of any return, . . . determining the liability of *any* person . . . or collecting *any* such liability . . ." [emphasis added].

Therefore, unless a court finds that the records in question are not relevant to a legitimate tax investigation or are not adequately described in the summons, or that the summons itself was too broad or improperly served, these taxpayer challenges will fail.

Until Congress passed the Reform Act, "John Doe" summonses required no pre-issuance court review. Now they may be served only *after* a court proceeding is held in which the Internal Revenue Service establishes (1) that the summons relates to the investigation of a particular person or a definable class of persons; (2) that there is reason to believe that this person or group may fail or have failed to comply with the tax law; and (3) that the data being sought from the records in question as well as the identity of the suspected tax law violators, are not readily available from other sources. In short, the law rules out "fishing expeditions."

Furthermore, the Reform Act requires the Internal Revenue Service to issue regulations setting out conditions under which banks and other institutions can be reimbursed for the cost of complying with one of these summonses.

After 63 years, the Tax Reform Act of 1976 finally excuses the taxpayer for errors made in writing *by the Internal Revenue Service*. Until the Act went into effect, even if a tax return had been prepared by the Internal Revenue Service, interest on any underpayment was charged from the original due date of the return. Now, if the IRS incorrectly prepares the return, the agency must wait a month after notifying the taxpayer and demanding payment before it may begin to charge any interest.

If an IRS employee makes an error in giving the taxpayer advice orally, interest is still charged from the due date of the return, since the taxpayer can't prove the agency misled him. In fiscal 1976, the Internal Revenue service answered questions and prepared returns for over 38 million taxpayers who either telephoned or visited an IRS office. The moral to this story is "get it in writing."

The Tax Reform Act of 1976 was also an attempt to respond to the outcries against administrative misuse of the jeopardy and termination assessments. These assessments had allowed the Internal Revenue Service at any time to collect taxes it said a taxpayer owed. There was no administrative or judicial review of the appropriateness or reasonableness of the assessments and the taxpayer immediately lost the use of his property. In fact, until 1976, the Internal Revenue Service took the position that it had "no obligation to prove that the seizure has any basis in fact, no matter how severe or irreparable the injury to the taxpayer and no matter how inadequate his eventual remedy in the Tax Court." This attitude invited agent abuse and inspired taxpayer paranoia.

The Reform Act sought to add balance to the scales of justice by matching the Internal Revenue Service's accelerated assessment power with a newly created taxpayer right to speed up review. Within five days after the jeopardy or termination assessment, the Internal Revenue Service must now give the taxpayer a written statement of the information on which it bases the assessment. The taxpayer then has 30 days in which to demand an administrative review of the propriety of this assessment action. The Internal Revenue Service must complete this review within 15 days and if the agency finds the assessment inappropriate or excessive in amount, it may reduce or eliminate it entirely.

If the taxpayer is not satisfied with the result of this review, he has 30 days in which to file suit in his local Federal District Court. Within 20 days, the court must make a new, independent determination as to whether the assessment was reasonable and whether the amount assessed was appropriate. In this proceeding, the Internal Revenue Service must prove that making the assessment was reasonable under the circumstances and must give the taxpayer a written statement setting out its basis for the dollar amount assessed. The taxpayer, though, still has the burden of proving that this dollar amount is unreasonable.

The writers of the Reform Act hoped that this quick administrative and judicial review would remove the temptation to misuse the special assessment process in tax collection and thereby safeguard the property of the innocent taxpayer. These assessments still conflict with our basic constitutional doctrine that the citizen is innocent until proven guilty. But that is a fault of our tax laws, not our tax administrators. Our revenue laws consistently take the position that all deductions are disallowed until proven, that the American taxpayer is cheating (guilty) until he can prove otherwise.

Finally, the Tax Reform Act of 1976 shattered the Internal Revenue Service's shield of secrecy, which had already been cracked by the 1974 amended Freedom of Information Act. Until the Reform Act went into effect, the IRS would issue private rulings and technical advice memoranda to individual taxpayers at their request. These "letter rulings" would answer specific taxpayer questions as to the tax effect of certain proposed actions. They would be administratively binding on the Internal Revenue Service, at least for the taxpayer who requested the advice. Letter rulings could not be used as precedent: the IRS could, and often did, take a completely contrary position with a different taxpayer in exactly the same situation or even with the same taxpayer if the situation arose again. The Internal Revenue Service could defend its switch with a candid admission that the first ruling was in error or that administrative interpretations had changed. Or the defense could be as simple as that the request went to two different Internal Revenue Service employees who disagreed in their application of the tax code. Remember, our tax law has a history of clarity that has often found four out of our nine Supreme Court Justices getting the wrong answer.

The problem with these private rulings and advice memorandum was that they were private. Since most of them were never published, they constituted a secret compilation of Internal Revenue Service administrative interpretations of our tax law. Only those that IRS administrators chose (in their unlimited discretion) to make public were available. These few were a small percentage of the total. While they could not be of value as precedents, they would clearly have worth as guidelines.

Internal Revenue Service arguments against the publication of these private rulings were many. Initially, the agency said it feared that expanded publication would slow down the procedure. Second, IRS officials argued, third parties could not rely on these rulings anyway. Furthermore, if letter rulings were to be made public, the agency believed that many taxpayers would be reluctant to seek advance rulings because of the prospective loss of privacy.

Martin Ginsburg, Chairman of the Tax Section of the New York State Bar Association, best summed up the conflict in his November 6, 1975, testimony before the Senate subcommittee hearings on Public Inspection of Internal Revenue Service Private Letter Rulings:

The . . . controversy over publication of private ruling letters reflects a tension between competing policies. On the one hand, there is the public's right to know: its right to know the law—to have assurance that there does not exist a body of "secret law"—and to know that the law is being applied with an even hand—to have assurance that the rich and the powerful are not the beneficiaries of an affirmative action program sponsored by the Internal Revenue Service. Ranked on the other side are concerns of personal privacy, trade secrets, business confidentiality, and more. Sensitivity to these concerns is heightened by a growing awareness that confidentiality of tax return information has been substantially eroded in recent years, and a manifest intention on the part of an increasing number of senators and representatives to reverse this trend.

The Tax Reform Act of 1976 provided that, as of November 1, 1976, anyone could see any written determination issued by the Internal Revenue Service, as well as any background file document relating to it. However, to balance the taxpayer's need for privacy against the public's need to know, the Act exempts from disclosure the individual taxpayer's identification and any confidential information contained in his request for a ruling.

Before disclosure, the Internal Revenue Service must delete trade secrets, privileged or confidential commercial or financial information, and "information the disclosure of which would be an unwarranted invasion of personal privacy," such as the report of a serious illness or pending divorce. The standard of care to be applied to the Internal Revenue Service's system for "sanitizing" these private rulings is that of "a reasonable man." The U.S. Court of Claims can award the injured taxpayer damages if the IRS fails to meet this standard. Court costs and a *minimum* award of $1,000 may be awarded if the court finds that the failure to delete was intentional.

Though most of the Tax Reform Act of 1976 is a labyrinth of convoluted and little understood "simplifications" of our substantive tax rules, it must be admitted that the Act did remedy many taxpayer–IRS administrative conflicts. In that area, at least, it may correctly be titled a "reform" act.

# 12/DOES THE END JUSTIFY THE MEANS?

What then are we left with?

Clearly the Internal Revenue Service has matured into a bureaucracy and like all bureaucracies it has developed a soul, a life, that transcends that of its employees. A true bureaucrat is an individual who has lost sight of the underlying purpose of the job at hand. One example might be the librarian whose concept of perfection is a well-stocked library with every book in its place. Readers, those who remove books, who disrupt the neatness and order of the system, are this librarian's natural enemies. He or she has forgotten that the fundamental purpose of a library is to facilitate the reading of books.

Consider the nurse at a large hospital who "must" know

an injured person's Blue Cross number before admitting him as a patient. This nurse has forgotten that the purpose of the hospital is to cure patients, not to make money. The means, the routines originally designed to serve the ends, have displaced the ends. To a true bureaucrat, the means become the ends.

What is the primary purpose of the Internal Revenue Service? It is to enforce our tax laws. It is not simply to collect *additional* taxes or to fight organized crime. It is to work for the American public, not keep secrets from it. It is to serve all of the American public, not just those powerful politicians who may command its administrators. If the true purpose of the Internal Revenue Service is to enforce our tax laws, should the auditor not work just as hard to refund overpaid taxes as he does to assess additional taxes? Should the auditor not receive as much "credit" for finding "no change" as he does for discovering a $1 million deficiency?

IRS policy, unfortunately, does not reflect the basis for the agency's existence. Employees have come to believe that their duty is to collect the tax, not to enforce the law. Perhaps this is due to poor communication between management and employees. Perhaps it is because neither management nor employees really believe they're expected simply to enforce the tax law. Perceived policy becomes procedure, and eventually procedure itself becomes policy. Bureaucrats do not serve jeopardy and termination summonses on people; they follow established procedure according to policy as determined by the application of relevant circumstantial criteria. Rote becomes revered over reason and taxpayers lose their humanity and become "cases." With Proper Utilization of Time (PUT), the Internal Revenue Service bureaucrat maximizes his success by disposing of "cases." This is a far cry from what his main duty should be: the correct determination of a taxpayer's tax liability.

Other bureaucracies do their job without prompting complaints of the quantity and intensity of those the Internal Revenue Service receives. Perhaps the agency's prominence as a special target of citizen criticism stems from its annual direct impact on every American taxpayer. Its existence and its effect hit home each week, every time the worker making $250 takes home only $200. The businessman or the professional remembers the IRS every time he makes another of the endless records needed to substantiate expenses as deductions. The power of the Internal Revenue Service is unmatched by any other domestic government agency except perhaps the Federal Bureau of Investigation. With its use of jeopardy and termination assessments, the Internal Revenue Service can destroy an individual both financially and emotionally without warning and, until recently, without effective judicial review.

While the existence of this special police power and the taxpayer's constant daily awareness of the financial burden of federal taxes have combined to shape the Internal Revenue Service, we cannot really understand the true nature of the agency, especially as a bureaucracy, in a vacuum, separate from the dictates of the tax laws. The Internal Revenue Service as an institution stems from these laws. It is their complexity, their ambiguity, that creates and allows the continued existence of an agency condemned for uneven, unclear, and at times even contradictory tax enforcement between districts and often between agents in the same office. As one auditor interviewed put it, "all agent decisions are subjective."

Citicorp Chairman Walter B. Wriston commented, "All the Congress, all the accountants and tax lawyers, all the judges and a convention of wizards cannot tell for sure what the income tax law says. Add to the laws the mass of regulations with the force of law, and the sheer weight of the imperatives brings voluntary compliance past the breaking point." Wriston is right. Given these laws, how can anyone expect anything like consistent, professional, and effective service from an agency staffed, as is the Internal Revenue Service, with mere mortals?

What exactly is our code of tax commandments? Clearly its function is more than just to finance the direct efforts of our federal government. In fact, according to political commentator George F. Will, the tax law is "a thicket of incentives and disincentives designed to get people to behave in ways considered socially useful."

Our tax code encourages millions of Americans to own homes by allowing the deduction of interest paid on a home mortgage, but not permitting the deduction of rent. It has been used to alleviate the economic impact of major illness by allowing taxpayers to deduct certain medical expenses. The dividend exclusion was added to foster the ownership of stock by small investors, and the investment tax credit has encouraged American industry to increase its productive capacity and create more jobs. Through Domestic International Sales Corporations, the tax law had encouraged manufacture at home rather than abroad by U.S. companies selling in foreign markets. It has encouraged investment in real estate developments, for example by permitting accelerated depreciation of new projects. Today, the energy crisis is being attacked through tax incentives and penalties.

Congress has used the tax code to indirectly finance projects it believes should be supported. For example, instead of directly granting millions of dollars to specific charities, Congress indirectly finances them by allowing a tax deduction for charitable contributions. The deduction of interest paid on a home mortgage is merely a hidden way for Congress to support and help finance the home real estate market. The list of these Congressional "tax expenditures" is endless. (see Table 3) The traditional tax deduction for the three martini, hundred dollar lunch could be considered one way of subsidizing the restaurant industry. Hotels and airlines receive hidden Congressional subsidies when businessmen can deduct convention travel and entertainment expenses.

Our tax code is the result of continuous and effective lobbying by individual pressure groups, each with its own extraordinary need and reason to be granted special beneficial tax legislation, effectively a hidden subsidy.

One might imagine the public outcry if the money lost through these "loopholes" in our tax structure were instead spent openly through direct Congressional expenditures. For example, the tax exclusion of scholarships and fellowships is the equivalent of direct government grants of $200 million, the exclusion of interest for state and local debt the equivalent of the federal government giving away $4.5 billion. The Committee on the Budget of the United States Senate estimated that these "tax expenditures" cost the U.S. Treasury $102.4 billion in 1977 alone. (Table 3) On February 13, 1978, Senator Edmund S. Muskie (D.-Me.) revealed that 31 percent of these tax benefits authorized for individuals through the tax code, go to only 1.4 percent of the U.S. taxpayers—those who make more than $50,000 a year. Perhaps these grants should be made, but not through the tax system. Make them in the open, as part of the U.S. budget, where the American public can clearly see their cost and weigh their appropriateness.

The American tax system also seeks to restructure our society by making the tax burden on upper income taxpayers greater than that on lower income citizens. It attempts to do this by collecting 70¢ out of every dollar beyond $102,200 a single taxpayer earns from rent, capital gains, sale of assets, and similar "unearned income," but only 14¢ out of each dollar earned between $2,200 and $2,700. This system is known as the progressive income tax. It does not work. Taxpayers wealthy enough to be in the 70% bracket have the funds and financial sophistication to employ lobbyists—professional merchants of congressional tax counsel—to solicit for them specific individual benefits, or they

## TABLE 3

### Estimated Revenue Loss Through Tax Expenditures
*(Millions of Dollars)*

| | 1975 | | 1976 | | 1977 | |
|---|---|---|---|---|---|---|
| | *Indiv.* | *Corp.* | *Indiv.* | *Corp.* | *Indiv.* | *Corp.* |
| Education, Training, Employment, and Social Services: | | | | | | |
| 5-year amortization of child care facilities .............. | — | 5 | — | 5 | — | 5 |
| Exclusion of scholarships and fellowships ............... | 200 | — | 210 | — | 220 | — |
| Parental personal exemption for student age 19 or over ......... | 670 | — | 690 | — | 715 | — |
| Deductibility of charitable contributions | | | | | | |
| Educational institutions .......... | 440 | 205 | 450 | 215 | 500 | 280 |
| Institutions other than educational . | 4385 | 385 | 3820 | 395 | 3955 | 525 |
| Deductibility of child and dependent care services ............... | 295 | — | 330 | — | 420 | — |
| Credit of employing public assistance recipients under Work Incentive (WIN) Program ............... | — | 10 | — | 10 | — | 10 |

Health:

| | | | | | | |
|---|---|---|---|---|---|---|
| Exclusion of employer contributions to medical insurance premiums and medical care .... | 3275 | — | 3665 | — | 4225 | — |
| Deductibility of medical expenses .... | 2315 | — | 2020 | — | 2095 | — |

Income Security:

| | | | | | | |
|---|---|---|---|---|---|---|
| Exclusion of Social Security benefits (disability insurance benefits, OASI benefits for the aged, and benefits for dependents and survivors) .... | 3465 | — | 3855 | — | 4460 | — |
| Exclusion of railroad retirement benefits .... | 170 | — | 185 | — | 200 | — |
| Exclusion of sick pay .... | 315 | — | 330 | — | 350 | — |
| Exclusion of unemployment insurance benefits .... | 2300 | — | 3305 | — | 2855 | — |
| Exclusion of worker's compensation benefits .... | 505 | — | 555 | — | 640 | — |
| Exclusion of public assistance benefits | 105 | — | 115 | — | 130 | — |
| Net exclusion of pension contributions and earnings: | | | | | | |
| Employer plans .... | 5215 | — | 5745 | — | 6475 | — |
| Plans for self-employed and others .. | 390 | — | 770 | — | 965 | — |

## TABLE 3 (con't)

| | 1975 Indiv. | 1975 Corp. | 1976 Indiv. | 1976 Corp. | 1977 Indiv. | 1977 Corp. |
|---|---|---|---|---|---|---|
| Exclusion of other employee benefits: | | | | | | |
| Premiums on group term life insurance | 740 | — | 805 | — | 895 | — |
| Premiums on accident and accidental insurance | 50 | — | 55 | — | 60 | — |
| Privately financed supplementary unemployment benefits | 5 | — | 5 | — | 5 | — |
| Meals and lodging | 265 | — | 285 | — | 305 | — |
| Exclusion of interest on life insurance savings | 1545 | — | 1695 | — | 1855 | — |
| Exclusion of capital gains on house sales if over 65 | 40 | — | 45 | — | 50 | — |
| Deductibility of casualty losses | 280 | — | 300 | — | 330 | — |
| Excess percentage standard deduction over low income allowance | 1385 | — | 1465 | — | 1560 | — |
| Additional exemption for the blind | 30 | — | 20 | — | 25 | — |
| Additional exemption for over 65 | 1100 | — | 1155 | — | 1220 | — |
| Retirement income credit | 130 | — | 120 | — | 110 | — |
| Earned income credit | N.A. | — | 1455 | — | 1390 | — |
| Maximum tax on earned income | 400 | — | 480 | — | 580 | — |

## Veterans' Benefits and Services:

| | | | | | | |
|---|---|---|---|---|---|---|
| Exclusion of disability compensation, pensions, and GI bill benefits ...... | 820 | — | 950 | — | 905 | — |

## General Government:

| | | | | | | |
|---|---|---|---|---|---|---|
| Credits and deductions for political contributions ................. | 40 | — | 40 | — | 65 | — |

## Revenue Sharing and General Purpose Fiscal Assistance:

| | | | | | | |
|---|---|---|---|---|---|---|
| Exclusion of interest on state and local bond debt ................. | 1130 | 2675 | 1280 | 2890 | 1390 | 3150 |
| Exclusion on income earned in U.S. possessions ................. | — | 245 | — | 240 | — | 285 |
| Deductibility of nonbusiness state and local taxes (other than on owner-occupied homes and gasoline) ...... | 8490 | — | 6505 | — | 6680 | — |

## National defense:

| | | | | | | |
|---|---|---|---|---|---|---|
| Exclusion of benefits and allowances to armed forces ................. | 650 | — | 650 | — | 650 | — |
| Exclusion of military disability pensions ................. | 70 | — | 80 | — | 90 | — |

TABLE 3 (con't)

| | 1975 Indiv. | 1975 Corp. | 1976 Indiv. | 1976 Corp. | 1977 Indiv. | 1977 Corp. |
|---|---|---|---|---|---|---|
| **International Affairs:** | | | | | | |
| Exclusion of gross-up on dividends of less developed country corporations | — | 55 | — | 55 | — | 55 |
| Exclusions of certain income earned abroad by U.S. citizens | 130 | — | 145 | — | 160 | — |
| Deferral of income of Domestic International Sales Corporation (DISCs) | — | 1130 | — | 1340 | — | 1420 |
| Special rates for Western Hemisphere Trade Corporations | — | 50 | — | 50 | — | 50 |
| Deferral of income of controlled foreign corporations | — | 590 | — | 525 | — | 365 |
| **Agriculture:** | | | | | | |
| Expensing of certain capital outlays | 475 | 135 | 355 | 105 | 360 | 115 |
| Capital gain treatment of certain income | 455 | 30 | 490 | 30 | 565 | 40 |
| **Natural Resources, Environment, and Energy:** | | | | | | |
| Expensing of intangible drilling, exploration and development costs | 120 | 500 | 155 | 650 | 195 | 840 |

| | | | | | | |
|---|---|---|---|---|---|---|
| Excess of percentage over cost depletion | 465 | 2010 | 500 | 1080 | 575 | 1020 |
| Capital gain treatment of royalties on coal and iron ore | 40 | 10 | 45 | 15 | 50 | 20 |
| Timber: Capital gains treatment of certain income | 60 | 145 | 60 | 155 | 65 | 165 |
| Pollution control: 5-year amortization | — | 30 | — | 20 | — | 15 |
| **Commerce and Transportation:** | | | | | | |
| Corporate surtax exemption | — | 3345 | — | 5015 | — | 6185 |
| Deferral of tax on shipping companies | — | 70 | — | 105 | — | 130 |
| Railroad rolling stock: 5-year amortization | — | 55 | — | 30 | — | 10 |
| Bad debt deductions of financial institutions in excess of actual losses | — | 880 | — | 815 | — | 570 |
| Deductibility of nonbusiness state gasoline taxes | 820 | — | 575 | — | 600 | — |
| Depreciation in excess of straight line: | | | | | | |
| Rental housing | 405 | 115 | 430 | 120 | 455 | 125 |
| Buildings other than rental housing | 220 | 220 | 215 | 275 | 215 | 280 |
| Expensing of research and development costs | — | 635 | — | 660 | — | 695 |
| Investment tax credit | 950 | 4860 | 1410 | 6850 | 1530 | 7585 |

TABLE 3 (con't)

| | 1975 | | 1976 | | 1977 | |
|---|---|---|---|---|---|---|
| | Indiv. | Corp. | Indiv. | Corp. | Indiv. | Corp. |
| Asset depreciation range .............. | 140 | 1870 | 155 | 1435 | 175 | 1630 |
| Dividend exclusion ................ | 315 | — | 335 | — | 350 | — |
| Capital gains: Individual (other than farming and timber) ........... | 5090 | — | 5455 | — | 6225 | — |
| Capital gains treatment: Corporate (other than farming and timber) ... | — | 695 | — | 760 | — | 900 |
| Exclusion of capital gains at death ..... | 6450 | — | 6720 | — | 7280 | — |
| Deferral of capital gains on home sales | 805 | — | 845 | — | 890 | — |
| Deductibility of mortgage interest and property taxes on owner-occupied property ...................... | 9915 | — | 8235 | — | 8535 | — |
| Exemption of credit unions ........... | — | 115 | — | 125 | — | 135 |
| Deductibility of interest on consumer credit .......................... | 1185 | — | 1040 | — | 1075 | — |
| Credit for purchasing a new home .... | — | — | 625 | — | 100 | — |
| Community and Regional Development: Housing rehabilitation: 5-year amortization ......................... | 65 | 40 | 55 | 35 | 40 | 25 |
| TOTAL | 69,310 | 20,510 | 71,280 | 24,002 | 74,810 | 26,630 |

are smart enough to hire professional tax planners to shelter their potentially taxable income. In either case the result is the same: only the ignorant rich are trapped by the 70% brackets. The bulk of the tax revenue comes from the middle class. Taxpayers in this group earn enough to be hurt by the progressive bracket structure but not enough to afford sophisticated planning and shelters. Taxation based upon ability to pay is a fiction, a fairy tale told but no longer believed.

Almost all tax experts agree that the United States Internal Revenue Code is far too complicated. This nightmarish complexity, the real cause of many inconsistencies in administration, of much taxpayer resentment of the IRS, and to some degree of the tax revolt now brewing across the nation, is in large part the result of Congress' efforts to use the tax code as a tool in trying to solve almost all of our national problems. Former Internal Revenue Service Commissioner Donald C. Alexander commented in July, 1977:

Our Internal Revenue Code has become too complicated to serve as a sound vehicle for the imposition of a broad-based income tax. . . . Making our system simple and understandable is more important than trying to attain every social and economic objective perceived at the time to be worthwhile.

Treasury Secretary W. Michael Blumenthal agreed. In a September 1977 speech before the American Institute of Certified Public Accountants, he said, "The system is far too complex. And we can no longer accept this complexity as a necessary price we pay for achieving important social goals. We can—and will—reduce tax complexity because it has become a major source of inequity—and because tax simplicity is itself a social good." Secretary Blumenthal was blunt in his evaluation of the tax code. "The income tax code today, to the average American, is a mystery," he told the American Institute of Public Accountants. Yet he and the current administration continue to use the tax code in their plans to stimulate investment and savings, create incentives to work, and increase growth and efficiency in the economy.

The original goal of the tax code, to raise revenue to finance our government and its direct expenditures, was eclipsed long ago. If the goals are complex, unclear, and at times contradictory—for example, to stimulate the economy with a general tax cut while at the same time increasing Social Security taxes because that's "a different system" —how can the administrator of the laws made to reach these goals, the Internal Revenue Service, be expected to function smoothly and efficiently? Tax administration within a system of uncertainty will itself be uncertain. If the laws are too complicated to be clearly understood and followed, the system, of necessity, becomes unmanageable.

An Internal Revenue Service employee was asked what effect the income tax had on our society: was it doing us harm?

I think so, and so do a lot of other people in and out of the Internal Revenue Service. I don't want to use the word corruption because that implies a moral judgment that I am not prepared to make. I can't blame taxpayers for cheating and when I catch them doing it, I deliver no sermons. What bothers me about the phenomenon of tax-dodging is not the morally corrupting effect, if any, but the enormous national waste of energy and good brain power. In our present set up, man's inventive and creative energies are twisted in the wrong direction—call it corruption if you will. If any inventive man must devote much of his brain power to the problem of avoiding or evading taxes on his company's income—this brings little benefit to society.

It becomes a game of beat the system, avoid the tax. People buy houses not because they want to live in them but because the interest is deductible. Charitable contributions are made not out of generosity but for tax write-offs. Business decisions are made not on the basis of profitability or market share but because of potential tax consequences. A champion fighter refuses a match because he is in too high a tax bracket this year. Tax effects have preempted the purpose of living.

# SELECTED
# BIBLIOGRAPHY

Bittker, Boris I., *Federal Income, Estate and Gift Taxation,*
Little, Brown, Boston: 1964.
Chodorov, Frank, et al., *Income Tax,* revised edition, Devin-
Adair Company, Old Greenwich, Connecticut: 1959.
Chommie, John C., *The Internal Revenue Service,* Praeger
Publishers, New York: 1970.
Chommie, John C., *Federal Income Taxation,* West Publish-
ing Co., St. Paul, Minn.: 1968.
Commerce Clearing House, *Tax Reform Act of 1976,* Chi-
cago: 1976.
Cushman, Robert E., and Cushman, Robert F., editors, *Cases
in Constitutional Law,* third edition, Appleton-Century-
Crofts, New York: 1968.

Diogenes, *The April Game,* Playboy Press, Chicago, Ill.: 1973.

Doris, Lillian, editor, *The American Way in Taxation: Internal Revenue 1862–1963,* Prentice-Hall, Inc., Englewood Cliffs, New Jersey: 1963.

Flower, Lenore E., *Visit of President George Washington to Carlisle, 1794,* Hamilton Library and Cumberland County Historical Society, Carlisle, Pa.: 1932.

Hacker, Andrew, Introduction to *The Federalist Papers,* Washington Square Press, New York: 1971.

Irey, Elmer, *The Tax Dodgers,* Greenberg, New York: 1948.

Joint Tax Program. *Problems of Tax Administration in Latin America,* Johns Hopkins Press, Baltimore: 1965.

Kaufman, Richard F., *The War Profiteers,* The Bobbs-Merril Co., Inc., Indianapolis, Indiana: 1971; Doubleday & Company, Inc., Garden City, New York: 1972.

Kendall, Willmoore and Carey, George W., *The Federalist Papers,* Introduction by Wilmoore Kendall, Arlington House, Inc., New Rochelle, New York.

Larson, Martin A., *Tax Revolt USA,* Liberty Lobby paperback, Washington, D.C.: 1973.

Lundberg, Ferdinand, *The Rich and the Super-Rich: A Study in the Power of Money Today,* Lyle Stuart, Inc., Secaucus, New Jersey: 1968.

Mellon, Andrew W., *Taxation: The People's Business,* MacMillan, New York: 1924.

Mertens, Jacob, Jr., *The Law of Federal Income Taxation,* Vol. 9, Callaghan, Mundelein, Ill.: 1965.

Messick, Hank, *Secret File,* Putnam's, New York: 1969.

Mises, Ludwig von, *Human Action: A Treatise on Economics,* third revised edition, Henry Regnery Company, Chicago: 1966.

———, *Bureaucracy,* Arlington House, Inc., New Rochelle, New York: 1969, reprint of 1944 edition.

North, Douglas C., and Miller, Roger Leroy, *The Economics*

*of Public Issues*, Harper & Row, Publishers, New York: 1971.

Oldman, Oliver, et al. *Manual of Income Tax Administration.* Harvard Law School International Program in Taxation, Cambridge: 1967 (mimeo).

Paul, Randolph E., *Taxation in the United States*, Little, Brown, Boston: 1954.

Raby, William L. and Riblet, Carl, Jr., *The Reluctant Taxpayer*, Cowles Book Co., Inc., New York: 1970.

Ratner, Sidney. *Taxation and Democracy in America*, Wiley, New York: 1967.

Rothbard, Murray N. *What Has Government Done to Our Money?* pamphlet, Rampart College, Santa Ana, California: 1963.

Stern, Philip M., *The Rape of the Taxpayer*, Random House, New York: 1973.

Surface, William, *Inside Internal Revenue*, Coward, McCann & Geoghegan, Inc., New York: 1967.

Surrey, Stanley S., and William C. Warren, *Federal Income Taxation, Cases and Materials*, Foundation Press, Brooklyn: 1962.

## Articles

Acree, Vernon D. "From the Thoughtful Tax Man." *Taxes*, 40:73 (1962).

Aubry, Arthur S., Jr. "The Alcohol and Tobacco Tax Division." *Police*, Jan.–Feb., 1968.

Bacon, Donald W. "Ethical Considerations in Federal Tax Administration." *Taxes*, 41:74 (1963).

———. "Internal Revenue Service Policy Concerning Reopening of Closed Cases." *Tax Lawyer*, 22:659 (1969).

———. "Taxing Foreign Income of United States Taxpayers." *Taxes*, 43:362 (1965).

———. "The New Changes Taking Place in the Office of International Operations." *J. Taxation*, 24:361 (1965).

Balter, Harry G. "How the Office of International Operations Enforces U.S. Taxes in Foreign Countries." *J. Taxation,* 24:356 (1965).

Barron, Dean J. "How We Audit from Magnetic Tapes." *Taxes,* 40:83 (1962).

——. "The Processing Cycle: What Happens from Filing Date to Action Date." *J. Taxation,* 24:306 (1966).

Barron, John. "The Tragic Case of John J. Hafer and the IRS." *Reader's Digest,* Jan., 1969.

——. "Time for Reform in the IRS." *Reader's Digest,* Sept., 1968.

——. "Tyranny in the Internal Revenue Service." *Reader's Digest,* Aug., 1967.

Belz, Saul C. "Federal Tax Rulings: Procedure and Policy." *Vanderbilt Law Review,* 21:78 (1967).

Blum, Walter J. "Nonaggression Revisited in a Nutshell—A Satirical View of Mr. Wormser's Plea." *J. Taxation,* 20:186 (1964).

Brazill, Clarence P., Jr. "The Audit Trail." *New York Univ. Tax Inst.,* 21:1217 (1963).

Caplin, Mortimer M. "The Commissioner's Reply: Reasonable Tax Administration and Current Policies of IRS." *J. Taxation,* 20:110 (1964).

Chamberlin, Hope. "The IRS Information Program." *National Public Accountant,* April, 1965.

Christenson, Reo M. "Report on the *Reader's Digest.*" *Columbia Journalism Review,* Winter, 1965.

Cohen, Sheldon S. "Latin American Tax Improvement." *Accounting Forum,* May, 1968.

Collie, Marvin K., and Thomas P. Marinis, Jr. "Ethical Considerations on Discovery of Error in Tax Returns." *Tax Lawyer,* 22:455 (1969).

Conlon, Charles F. "Administration of the State Income Tax." *1962 Proceedings National Tax Assn.,* 1963, p. 404.

Eichel, Claude L. "Administrative Aspects of the Prevention

and Control of International Tax Evasion." *Miami Law Review*, 20:25 (1965).

Escew, Anne E., *et al.* "Lead Poisoning Resulting from Illicit Alcohol Consumption." *J. Forensic Sciences*, 6:337 (1961).

Farioletti, Marius. "Statistical Records for the Management and Control of Tax Administration." In *Problems of Tax Administration in Latin America*, Baltimore: Johns Hopkins Press, 1965, p. 112.

Fox, C. I. "Office of International Operations: What It Does and How It Functions." *J. Taxation*, 24:162 (1965).

Gould, Stephen. "A Case Study in Effective Recruitment." *Personnel Administration*, 25:31 (1962).

Grant, Irving M. "The Sierra Club: The Procedural Aspects of the Revocation of Its Tax Exemption." *UCLA Law Review*, 15:200 (1967).

Haberstroh, Chadarck J. "The Impact of Electronic Data Processing on Administrative Organizations." *National Tax J.*, 14:258 (1961).

Huston, Luther A. "IRS Leans on Press to Assist Taxpayers." *Editor and Publisher*, April 22, 1967.

Jack, Robert L. "ADP—An Analysis of Its Operations and Results." *New York Univ. Tax Inst.*, 24:99 (1966).

―――. "Man v. Machine: Routine Correspondence Now Carried on by IRS Computer." *J. Taxation*, 24:307 (1966).

Klotz, Arthur H. "Administrative Appeals—Avoiding Litigation." *Tax Executive*, 19:188 (1967).

Kragen, Adrian A. "The Private Ruling: An Anomaly of Our Internal Revenue System." *Taxes*, 45:331 (1967).

Lehrfeld, William J., and George D. Webster. "Administration by the IRS of Non-Profit Organization Tax Matters." *Tax Lawyer*, 21:591 (1968).

Link, David T. "RIRA—A Legal Information System in the Internal Revenue Service." *Taxes*, 43:231 (1965).

Machiz, Irving. "How the Internal Revenue Performs Its Review of the Revenue Agent's Report." *Taxation for Accountants*, 1:201 (1966).

Marrs, Aubrey R. "The Constitutional Power of Congress over the Administration of Federal Taxation." *Taxes*, 31: 503 (1953).

Miller, Ream V. "A Tax Representative's Appraisal of Tax Simplification and Uniform Tax Administration." *Tax Executive*, 17:7 (1964).

Miller, Richard S. "Administrative Agency Intelligence-Gathering: An Appraisal of the Investigative Powers of the Internal Revenue Service." *Boston College Industrial & Commercial Law Review*, 6:657 (1965).

Miller, Robert N. "The Reorganization of the Bureau of Internal Revenue—An Appraisal." *Taxes*, 30:967 (1952).

Montague, Edwin N. "Internal Revenue Service Training Program for Tax Men." *1959 Proceedings National Tax Assn.*, 1960, p. 124.

Moss, Harold. "Experience Under the U.S. Foreign Tax Assistance Program." *1967 Proceedings National Tax Assn.*, 1968, p. 392.

Packowski, George W. "Alcoholic Beverages, Distilled." In Kirk-Othmer, *Encyclopedia of Chemical Technology*, Vol. 1, New York: Wiley, 1963.

Penniman, Clara. "Reorganization and the Internal Revenue Service." *Public Administration Review*, 21:121 (1961).

————. "Selected Problems in State Income Tax Administration." *1955 Proceedings National Tax Assn.*, 1956.

Plumb, Robert C. "Report of Survey of Federal Audit Practices." *Tax Executive*, 16:214 (1964).

Ritholz, Jules. "The Commissioner's Inquisitorial Powers." *Taxes*, 45:331 (1967).

Rivers, Caryl. "IRS: They're Usually Honest With Newsmen." *Editor and Publisher*, April, 1964.

Robertson, Joseph M. "Recent Developments in Federal-State Cooperation." *1958 Proceedings National Tax Assn.*, 1959, p. 483.

Rogovin, Mitchell. "The Four R's: Regulations, Rulings, Reliance and Retroactivity." *Taxes*, 43:756 (1965).

Rosapepe, Joseph S. "How to Collect $155—Billion." *Public Relations Journal*, April, 1968.

Seghers, Paul D. "Federal Tax Reform: The Practitioner's Viewpoint." *1963 Proceedings National Tax Assn.*, 1964, p. 71.

Semling, Harold V., Jr. "Data Processing at the Internal Revenue Service." *Modern Data Systems*, Feb., 1968.

Smith, Dan Throop. "The Function of Tax Treaties." *National Tax J.*, 12:317 (1959).

Smith, William H. "Developing a New Technique in Selecting Returns for Audit." *J. Accountancy*, 123:22 (1967).

———. "Disciplinary Problems of the Service." *Tax Lawyer*, 22:255 (1969).

———. "Electronic Data Processing in the Internal Revenue Service." *National Tax J.*, 14:210 (1961).

Stillman, Don. "Attack on the Taxman." *Columbia Journalism Review*, Winter, 1967–68.

Stock, Leon O. "From the Thoughtful Tax Man." *Taxes*, 42:403 (1964).

Surrey, Stanley S. "Computer Technology and Federal Tax Policy." *National Tax J.*, 19:248 (1966).

Treusch, Paul E. "Chief Counsel's Office: A Dynamic View of Its Organization and Procedures: The 'Hows' and Something of the 'Whys.'" *So. Calif. Tax Inst.*, 12:19 (1960).

Turner, James R. "Federal-State Cooperation in Tax Administration." *William & Mary Law Review*, 9:958 (1968).

Uretz, Lester R. "Settlement of Tax Controversies." *Taxes*, 44:794 (1966).

Volpone, Stephen C. "How a Tax Controversy Is Handled at the Appellate Division Level." *J. Taxation*, 23:178 (1965).

Wormser, Rene A. "To the Commissioner of Internal Revenue: A Plea for 'Nonaggression.'" *J. Taxation*, 20:108 (1964).

### U.S. Government Printing Office Publications

Department of the Treasury. *Income Taxes 1862–1962: A History of the Internal Revenue Service*, 1962.
———. *Report of the Secretary of the Treasury*. Annual.
House Committee on Appropriations. Subcommittee on Treasury, Post Office, and Executive Office. *Annual Hearings*. Part 2, Treasury Department.
House Committee on Government Operations. *Federal Effort Against Organized Crime: Report of Agency Operations*, 1968.
House Committee on Ways and Means. *Treasury Department Report on Private Foundations*, 1965.
———. Subcommittee on Internal Revenue Taxation. *Progress Report*, 1957.
NOTE: The *Hearings* of both the House Ways and Means Committee and the Senate Committee on Finance frequently contain material on tax administration.
Internal Revenue Service. *Alcohol and Tobacco Tax Division*. Publication 425, 1966.
———. *Commissioner's Report to the Secretary of the Treasury*. Annual.
———. *Detection and Investigation of Attempted Criminal Violations of Tax Laws*. Document 5490, 1967.
———. *Dimensions of Personal Management*, 1967.
———. *Distilled Spirits: History of Taxation and Law Enforcement*. Document 5574, 1966.
———. *IRS Answers* Reader's Digest *Article; Gives Facts on Tax Cases Made Public*. Document 5958, 1967.
———. *IRS Audit Guide*, 1977.
———. "Statement of Organization and Functions." *Federal Register*, 34:1657, 1969.

Joint Committee on Internal Revenue Taxation, *Investigation into Certain Charges of the Use of the Internal Revenue Service for Political Purposes,* U.S.G.P.O., 1973.

Senate Committee on Finance, *Hearings on* H.R. 10612, U.S.G.P.O., 1976.

Senate Committee on Judiciary. Subcommittee on Administrative Practice and Procedure. *Hearings on Invasions of Privacy,* Parts 3, 4, and 5, 1965–66.

Senate Committee on Finance. Subcommittee on Administration of the Internal Revenue Code, *Hearings on the Role of the IRS in Law Enforcement Activities,* U.S.G.P.O., 1976.

# INDEX

233